Finance

How to secure your financial future

Moira O'Neill

A & C Black • London

First published in the United Kingdom in 2008 by

A & C Black Publishers Ltd
38 Soho Square, London W1D 3HB
www.acblack.com

A CIP record for this book is available from the British Library.

ISBN: 9-781-408-10111-7

This book is produced using paper that is made from wood grown in
managed, sustainable forests. It is natural, renewable and recyclable.
The logging and manufacturing processes conform to the
environmental regulations of the country of origin.

Design by Fiona Pike, Pike Design, Winchester
Typeset by RefineCatch Ltd, Bungay, Suffolk
Printed in the United Kingdom by CPI Bookmarque, Croydon

Contents

CONTENTS

About the author

Moira O'Neill has been a personal finance journalist for 11 years. Six of these were spent writing articles about saving and investing for an over-40s readership at *Money Observer* magazine, where she was deputy editor. At the same time, she was also personal finance editor of *Guardian Weekly*, the newspaper for British expatriates. She is currently personal finance editor at the *Investors Chronicle*.

Disclaimer

Information provided in this book is only for general information and use and is not intended to address your particular requirements. Independent professional financial advice should be obtained before making any investment decisions.

The value and income derived from investments can go down as well as up. Past performance cannot be relied upon as a guide to future performance.

All facts, figures and other data contained in this book have been obtained from sources believed to be reliable. Although carefully verified by the author, this information cannot be guaranteed by the author.

The author has made every effort to ensure that facts and figures in this book were accurate at the time of writing. However, the financial world changes very quickly and you should check current tax rates and allowances before making financial decisions.

Introduction

You're 40. You haven't yet given a thought to planning for your retirement. That's perfectly understandable, as your finances until now have probably concentrated on paying off debts, building a deposit to get on the property ladder, paying off your mortgage and perhaps supporting a growing family. But now that you're about halfway through life, it's time to bite the bullet and start planning for the future.

You may have seen your parents reach retirement. If they're part of the 'Baby Boomer' generation – the first tranche of which was born between 1946 and 1954 – they're probably sitting on decent pensions and valuable properties to tide them through their golden years. However, your experience is likely to be different.

Bad luck: things are much more difficult for your generation. State pensions are diminishing and private pensions are no longer gold-plated. So you'll have to take on much more personal responsibility for your retirement plans. NOW is the time to start planning for your golden years, if you want them to be golden and not miserable. Forty isn't too late – in fact, it's a very good age to start planning as you still have many years until state pension age, which will have risen to 66 by the time you retire.

Twenty-six years is plenty of time to stash away a decent amount. But if you delay, you may find that it's difficult to catch up. It's not going to be good enough to save money into your bank account. You're going to have to put it into the stock market – and this means you'll need to choose some stock market investments for your money.

You know nothing about investing? Most of your contemporaries know very little – although many are reluctant to admit this. But it will pay to learn the basics, and it's not as daunting as it may at first seem.

In the chapters that follow, I'll explain how to build up a portfolio of investments that you can rely on in future if you need an income or a lump sum.

How to read this book

My advice is don't try to read it in one go. Finance and investing are complicated and they could bring on a panic attack and leave you with palpitations! Digest slowly, taking one step at a time.

What this book won't do

Debt is obviously something that you need to deal with before you can start investing for a secure future. I'm not going to spend time addressing debt problems – that could be a whole book in itself – but you'll find useful contacts at the back of this book to help you overcome debt issues.

Am I alone?

'Everyone else seems to know so much about finances. And they're confident that they'll have enough to live on in retirement. I'm afraid to talk to my friends about my worries.'

The likelihood is you're not talking to your friends or family about your finances at all, as money has usurped politics as the greatest taboo conversation topic. Two-thirds of Brits feel money is a personal subject that should be kept private, according to research by personal finance website Fool.co.uk. The study highlights how reluctant most of us are to chat about our cash, and reveals that politics, religious beliefs, career concerns and even relationship problems are more favoured than money as topics of conversation these days.

The vast majority of people fail to save sufficiently for retirement, and many fail to save at all. Other things, such as paying off the mortgage, bringing up kids etc., simply take priority. If you begin to save now, you'll have a head start on most of your contemporaries. Most people regret not having done more to save in the past, but it's not worth beating yourself up. Remember splashing out on special treats such as meals out and holidays with fondness!

What happens if you don't save for retirement?

Could you survive on £124.05 a week, the minimum income that the government currently guarantees in retirement? Wouldn't this be a struggle? You'd be able to buy enough to eat, certainly, but this is hardly an income that will let you enjoy a lifestyle including holidays, the occasional meal out, running a decent car and so on. Not having to deal with this prospect is just one very good reason to put money aside for retirement by saving in the private sector.

Nonetheless, state retirement benefits are a good basis for retirement planning and need to be factored into your plan. The trouble with relying on them, however, is that they're likely to be worth a lot less when you reach retirement than they are today. The question is, are you prepared to gamble on whether you'll be receiving a decent state pension in 20 or 30 years' time?

Unfortunately, many experts predict a steady erosion of state pensions as UK demographics change. This is because the number of older people will increase relative to the number of young people. The Government Actuary's Department (GAD) expects the average age of the population to rise from 38.8 in 2000 to 42.6 in 2025.

The current state pension

The state pension is paid to pensioners out of National Insurance (NI) funds paid by people currently working, so as the proportion of workers decreases, it will be more difficult for the government to find the funds to pay the state pension at current levels. This means we could eventually see a substantial cut in benefits. Following recommendations by experts and lobby groups, the government has already agreed that the most sensible solution is to raise the state retirement age.

The state pension age is set by law and for those retiring in 2008 is 60 for a woman and 65 for a man. You can't get your state pension before state pension age, even if you retire from your employment before then. For women born on or after 6 April (the start of the tax year) 1950, state pension age will begin to increase from April 2010, so that by 2020 both men and women will have the same state pension age of 65.

However, the state pension age for both men and women is to increase from 65 to 68 between 2024 and 2046, with each change phased in over two consecutive years in each decade. The first increase, from 65 to 66, will be phased in between April 2024 and April 2026; the second, from 66 to 67, will be phased in between April 2034 and April 2036; and the third, from 67 to 68, between April 2044 and April 2046.

So if you're 40 in 2008, you'll get your state pension when you're 66.

There is a state pension age calculator at www.thepensionservice.gov.uk/resourcecentre/statepensioncalc.asp

Basic state benefits

In the tax year 2008/09, the full basic state pension is £90.70 a week for a single person and £145.05 for a couple, where one partner has no entitlement of their own.

Qualification for the basic state pension depends on your National Insurance contribution (NIC) record. To qualify for the full basic state pension you currently need to accumulate 44 years of NIC credits between the ages of 16 and 65. However, the government is reducing the number of qualifying years needed for a full basic state pension to 30 for people who reach state pension age on or after 6 April 2010.

There could be gaps in your NIC record if you have been:

- unemployed and not claiming benefit
- living abroad
- self-employed and exempt from paying Class 2 contributions

If you don't have the required NIC credits, you'll receive a smaller basic state pension based on the number of qualifying years you do have. From 2010, people who have fewer than 30 qualifying years will get 1/30 of full basic State Pension for each qualifying year they have. It is possible to make voluntary payments to make up a shortfall in NICs but you usually have to make up the shortfall within six years. For further information, contact the National Insurance Helpline for Individuals on 0845 302 1479 or write to National Insurance Contributions Office, Benton Park View, Newcastle upon Tyne, NE98 1ZZ.

Second state pension

There is a second state pension related to earnings, which can boost your retirement income by a small amount. The government has announced that between 2012 and 2015 the link with earnings will start to disappear, and the state second pension will start building up as a flat rate for each qualifying year. By 2030, it will become a fixed-rate pension regardless of earnings. Many people in occupational pension schemes (that is, pension schemes offered by their employer) contract out (opt out) of the second state pension and therefore pay reduced NICs as a result. However, from 2012 at the earliest, contracting out into certain types of private pension scheme will no longer be allowed.

Minimum income guarantee

If you've made no private pension provision, or have a gap in your NIC record, then you'll be struggling to make ends meet on what basic state pension you receive. However, the government has a safety net for poorer pensioners. It's called 'pension credit' and anyone with a NI number can apply for it.

Pension credit tops up retirement income to £124.05 a week for a single person and to £189.35 for a married couple (in tax year 2008/09). The amount you get is means-tested, so it will depend on your circumstances and any savings you already have. If you have more than £12,000 savings, you won't qualify. Also, the government looks at your other sources of retirement income, including any private pension due to you. However, pension credit has an element to reward the band of pensioners who have managed to save a little for retirement. If you have between £6,000 and £12,000 savings or a very small income from a private pension, you may qualify for this.

8

For further information contact the Pension Service on 0800 99 1234.

State pension forecast

You can get a state pension forecast, which will tell you in today's money the state pension you may get based on your NICs so far, and what you may get when you claim your state pension. It will also include details of your additional state pension, if you have one. Call the Future Pension Centre on 0845 3000 168, or write to the Future Pension Centre, The Pension Service, Tyneview Park, Whitley Road, Newcastle upon Tyne, NE98 1BA.

How much will you need to save?

Not wanting to be poor in your old age is a very good reason for having a long-term savings plan. You don't want to be cutting back your expenditure on clothing, heating, electricity and other essential bills, or making economies on food and drink. Many pensioners do just this to make ends meet.

The Friends Provident Freetirement Generation report, undertaken by social-trend researchers the Social Issues Research Centre, revealed that just 4 per cent of people in the UK feel they could live comfortably on the amount offered by the basic state pension, whereas seven in 10 people (69 per cent) – both those retired and still working – estimate they would need £600 or more a month to live comfortably.

Do you know that you'll need to stash away at least £150,000 to live comfortably on the interest in old age?

If at retirement you can – as now – get a 4 per cent return on your money, then £150,000 will produce an annual income of just £6,000, or £500 per month. Add the minimum state pension to this and you'll have a monthly income of about £600. If you get the maximum state pension, you'll have almost £900. Not enough to live in style, but certainly enough to live in comfort.

£150,000 may seem a frightening sum to save up, but it's very achievable on the UK's average annual gross salary for someone in their 40s of just under £27,000. (Median gross weekly earnings for full-time employees are £516 for 40 to 49 year olds. Source: National Statistics November 2007.) If you can find £200 a month to invest, this is well within your grasp. Assuming inflation at 4 per cent and a return on your investment of 7 per cent, this would grow to a pot of £176,204 by the time you reach 66, according to the calculator at the *Guardian*'s Money website (www.guardian.co.uk/money).

If you would like to achieve a retirement income equivalent to the average UK salary, which is around £24,000 a year, you need to build up a personal savings or company pension pot of around £360,000, or £500,000 if you want to 'inflation-proof' it, according to insurer Prudential.

Be realistic

Face it, you're probably not going to retire in your 50s, and neither am I, although I'd like to. But perhaps if we save really, really hard, we may still be able to retire in our 60s. The truth is that many of us may have to work well into our 70s.

But there's no point in moaning about it. This is simply the price we have to pay for higher life expectancy, for which we should be thankful. According to the Government Actuary's Department, today's 40-year-old man living in the UK can expect to live to 79, and a 40-year-old woman can expect to live to 82. Retirement is becoming a much larger portion of life. Today's 65 year olds can expect to live until they're 82 (men) and 85 (women). That's the best part of 20 years in retirement.

Think, instead, about the option of working part-time in later life, so that your pension is a supplement to earnings, rather than something to rely on completely. Why should there be any magic age beyond which people expect not to do any work at all? It's not healthy to sit at home all day, especially without much money to spend.

We've been brought up with a very cut-and-dried view of retirement: one day you're working, the next you're the proud owner of a carriage clock pondering the prospect of 20 years of full-time leisure. The reality is much more blurred and it's likely to become even more so in the future. We need to address the 'cliff edge of retirement' – effectively transforming it into much more of a slope through job-sharing, part-time work and so on. In years to come, more of us perhaps will find ourselves well beyond the age of 60 or 65 and still generating a level of earned income.

Hopefully, by the time you retire, when the over-60s will make up a more significant part of the population (birth rates are dropping rapidly), there'll be more employers willing to take on older workers on a part-time or job-sharing basis. Working in retirement is a common trend. About a third (31 per cent) of retirees plan to spend a large proportion of their time working. Nearly a quarter (24 per cent) of Baby Boomers questioned as part of the Friends Provident Freetirement Generation report said they had the freedom to choose the work they wanted to do, while 22 per cent said they work for social contact and could now enjoy work without the stress and responsibility of the rat race.

The report found that Baby Boomers have high work expectations in retirement, including continuing to work but without the stress, becoming involved in charities and exploring new professions. They are casting aside the image of pensioners trying to buy back their youth by bungee-jumping or skydiving, and are choosing to continue working – but only doing work they want to and at their own pace.

Where do you start?

You probably already have some retirement plans in place, although you may not realise this. Have you been paying NICs, for example? Are you a member of your employer's pension scheme? Have you some savings in the bank? Has your home risen in value since you bought it? These can all form the basis of a retirement plan.

Find out what you *do* have in place. This might be more than you think. By the time you're 40, you've probably been employed for the best part of 20 years. You may also have a NI record of 24 years – it starts when you're 16. Therefore, at some point along the way you may have picked up state-pension rights and an employer-sponsored pension scheme. You'll also have been banking, and possibly saving. Perhaps you've bought a flat or house. Perhaps you have an ISA – an individual savings account. You may have insurance policies.

If you're a real financial novice, your finances are probably very disorganised. Don't despair: now's the time to sort everything out.

Your financial goals in order of priority

1 **Pay off expensive debt.** By expensive debt, I mean non-mortgage debt. There's no point starting to save if you have expensive debts hanging round your neck. Store cards are the worst culprits as they charge very high rates of interest. However, even if you have a normal credit card on a reasonable rate, it makes sense to pay this off before putting money aside in a savings account or investment. The reason for this is your money is unlikely to earn more as savings or investment than you're paying out in interest on the debt.

2 **Save enough cash to give you a financial 'buffer' in case of emergency.** If you lose your job, wreck your car or have a family emergency, you'll need some spare cash to tide you through for a while. Ideally, this should be 3-6 months' income and be easily accessible in a bank account. Over half of people in the UK have less than two months' salary tucked away in savings for a rainy day, according to research by Scottish Widows in 2007. This simply isn't enough.

3 **Make sure you have financial protection for your family.**
Put the right insurance in place so that if you're seriously injured or die,
your financial dependants will have enough to live on in comfort.

4 **Have a place where you can live mortgage- or rent-free by
the time you retire.** If you bought a UK property 10 years ago, you've
probably seen a handsome rise in its value. This may not necessarily
continue, but 10 years of mortgage down-payments is a great start to
your financial plan. Why? Because you're on target to be mortgage-free
when you retire, which means you won't need to save and invest so much
money to achieve your required standard of living in retirement. Even if
you buy a property now, you could have paid off the mortgage by the time
you reach retirement age.

5 **Invest enough money now to provide you with an income
in retirement.** Work out what you'll need to live on in retirement:
probably a half to two-thirds what you live on now because you probably
won't have the major expenses of mortgage repayments in retirement.
Bear in mind that many retired people are active and in good health. You
might need a lump sum to travel the world and live out other retirement
dreams.

Most people can achieve a very comfortable standard of
living on £15,000 a year in retirement. So this should be the
ideal figure to aim for. You're going to get some help to

achieve this figure from the state. The basic state pension is currently £90.70 a week (2008/09 tax year), which works out at £4716.40 a year. So that leaves just over £10,000 to achieve.

However, if you're aiming to retire at 66 (the age at which you'll get your state pension), remember that 26 years is a long time in politics. The state pension may be very different by then. And it might be worth a lot less. For this reason, many financial advisers recommend that people treat the state pension as a bonus, and advise them not to rely on receiving it at its current level.

So you're really looking to invest to achieve a private income of £15,000. This means that over the next 26 years you need to accumulate a 'retirement pot' of money that you'll be able to invest when you retire to achieve this income.

Let's say at retirement you put all your money in a bank or building society account and it earns 4 per cent interest after savings tax. Your retirement pot needs to be £375,000. This sounds like a huge amount but it's definitely achievable if you invest through tax-efficient investments such as pensions.

If you saved for 26 years and your money didn't grow at all, you'd need to save £1,200 a month to get a pot of £375,000. But if you're a higher-rate taxpayer and put your money in a pension, it will instantly benefit from income-tax relief of 40 per cent, so to get £1,200 in a pension every month, you'll only need to put in £720. However, you're also going to benefit from investment growth – hopefully of 7 per cent a year. And compound interest will boost your savings, too. This means you probably only need to save between £400 and £500 a month into a pension to get a final pot of £375,000.

The pensions calculator at financial advisers Hargreaves Lansdown's website (www.h-l.co.uk) estimates that over 26 years, a gross contribution of £700 a month could get you a retirement income of £15,000. So a basic-rate taxpayer would need to contribute £560 a month and a higher-rate taxpayer would need to put in £420.

In reality, you may need to save less than this as you may already have some savings in place. Also, at some point in the next 26 years, you may get a pay rise or a promotion and have more disposable income to put aside. You may also get an inheritance or a windfall at some point, which will help to boost your retirement pot.

Where to find the money to invest

Feeling that you don't have any spare cash – and so would find it impossible to save for retirement – is very easy. But you're sticking your head in the sand. It's important to act now to safeguard your future, so think hard about streamlining your finances to free up some money for savings.

The best thing to do with a 'retirement pot' is to make payments into it on a regular (i.e. monthly) and automatic basis. Set up a standing order or direct debit so that money is taken out of your bank account as soon as you get paid and before you start spending on everyday expenses.

Take control of your finances by looking at all the areas where you can save money. Try not to see this as a chore – it's actually an opportunity. By saving on your outgoings, you're really increasing your disposable income.

Be proactive, not reactive. Instead of cutting back on treats, why not take the opportunity to cut the cost of your basics throughout the year. Check you're getting the best rates on your gas and electricity, car insurance, home phone bill, broadband, mobile phone, credit card, personal loan and current account. You can use Internet services such as www.uSwitch.com, www.moneysupermarket.com and www.moneysavingsexpert.com to save hundreds of pounds a year on household bills and financial products.

If you can't save enough money through streamlining your finances and switching to better deals, you simply have to cut down on some of life's luxuries. If you're not saving for retirement, you're living beyond your means.

Here are some ideas:

ACTION TO STOP	Weekly saving	Monthly saving	Annual saving
20 cigarettes a day	£35	£152	£1,820
Daily takeaway coffee	£14	£61	£728
Weekly takeaway Chinese/Indian	£10	£43	£520
Foreign holiday	–	–	£1,000

In 2007, Halifax released research that showed the amounts of money that people spend over the course of their lives on everyday innocuous purchases such as a coffee on the way to work and DVD rentals. What this research demonstrates is that the average person will spend in excess of a staggering £150,000 over the course of their lifetime on what might be described as 'little luxuries' – that is, goods and services of a non-essential nature – when a portion of this money could be made available for investment and other, larger, purchases.

On average, over a period of 40 years the average working person will spend the following:

- morning coffee £20,000
- sandwich lunch £52,000
- a weekly entertainment magazine £3,100

19

- pizza for two once a week with one glass of wine each £46,000
- a couple of DVDs a month £12,500
- a can of fizzy drink £6,300
- a 'quick pint' after work twice a week £8,500

Obviously you don't have to give up all life's treats. But by buying one less DVD a month and perhaps making your sandwiches at home, you could very easily save enough to make a reasonable monthly investment into your retirement pot.

2 Financial advice

Many people find that retirement planning isn't something they can do on their own and they need to consult an expert. At some point, it's likely that you'll need to use the services of a financial adviser to help you with investment decisions. In fact, it's a good idea to visit a financial adviser when you first start thinking about planning for your retirement. This book will help you weigh up whether your financial adviser is any good.

Although there are an estimated 18,000 financial advisers in the UK, finding reliable quality advice isn't straightforward. There *are* some very good financial advisers out there, but the question is how to find one.

How can a financial adviser help?

'Financial adviser' is a broad term that covers bank personnel, high-street brokers, professional wealth managers and investment advisers. He or she might be able to do some or all of the following: recommend savings products, set up a retirement plan, arrange a mortgage or insurance policy, restructure your investments, give advice on the tax-efficiency of your portfolio or help with tax planning.

Most people seek straightforward advice on issues such as borrowing money, putting financial protection in place and how to start saving for the future. More knowledgeable financial consumers may be able to sort out these 'basics' themselves, but may need higher-level advice on, say, investment and retirement-planning issues.

It's quite common for people to get along just fine making financial decisions but suddenly find that they need the guiding hand of a professional, particularly as they get nearer to retirement.

What are the different types of financial adviser?

Getting the right type of financial advice is extremely important. Changes to the rules about financial advice mean the market is currently split into three types of advice, which makes things a bit confusing.

1 **TIED ADVISERS** can give advice on and recommend products from one company.
2 **MULTI-TIED ADVISERS** can give advice on and recommend products from a limited number of companies.
3 **INDEPENDENT FINANCIAL ADVISERS (IFAs)** can give advice on and recommend products from the whole market.

Each type of advice has its merits, but if you have a large

sum to invest or substantial family assets on which you need advice, you need the professional top end of the market – an independent financial adviser. In fact, some financial advisers require you to have a certain net worth before offering services. For example, they may only take on clients who have, aside from their main property, an investment portfolio worth £100,000. Or if you are starting investing from scratch, they may want you to be looking to invest at least £300 a month.

If you're seeking advice on retirement planning, you should definitely look for an 'independent' financial adviser, who can recommend products from the whole of the market. Independent advice should be higher-quality and therefore to your considerable benefit longer-term.

Choosing an independent financial adviser

Most people first ask a trusted friend or relative for a recommendation. You could also ask your accountant or solicitor, who should have a good idea of the best financial advisers in your local area. If neither of these options is available, use IFA Promotion's 'Find an IFA' service at www.unbiased.co.uk to find an IFA close to your home. There are other contacts at the end of this chapter. It makes sense to interview and evaluate several financial advisers – at least three – to find the one that's right for you. You'll find that the first session with an IFA is usually free of charge.

What qualifications does an IFA need to practise?

The minimum qualification an IFA needs is the Certificate in Financial Planning, a qualification offered by the Chartered Insurance Institute. This is equivalent to an A-level. However, many areas of financial advice can be very complicated and demand a higher level of knowledge. More specialist professional qualifications – equivalent to a university degree – are on offer for complicated areas such as pensions, tax planning, trusts and specialist investment. 'Chartered Financial Planner' and the similar-sounding 'Certified Financial Planner' are high professional qualifications to look for.

■ **CHARTERED FINANCIAL PLANNER** is a title awarded by the Chartered Insurance Institute to experienced financial advisers who have a level of qualification equivalent to a first degree. The adviser must have worked in the industry for at least five years, and have at least six Advanced Financial Planning Certificate level units or the equivalent. Bear in mind that it's one thing being a technical genius, but an adviser has to be able to relate this to a client's circumstances.

■ **CERTIFIED FINANCIAL PLANNER** is a similarly high-level qualification awarded by the Institute of Financial Planning but is more about the practical application of technical knowledge. It's a case-study-based exam which builds in report-based advice.

How do I pay for advice?

If an adviser has 'independent' status, he or she has to offer you the option of paying via a fee. You can also pay by commission on the products sold or agree on a mixture of fees and commission.

If you need advice on any less-than-straightforward matters, it's worth turning to the small but growing band of professional, fee-based advisers, who take no commission but get paid directly by the client for the ongoing advice they provide. The fact that these advisers work on a fee basis doesn't mean they're the best, of course, but it's a better start than the commission-based model. The big advantage of fees is that it makes it far more likely that the adviser will act with your best interests at heart. Fees mean there will be no conflict of interest and the adviser won't be tempted to recommend a product just because it pays him or her the biggest commission.

IFAs may also offer you the option of offsetting commissions on products against the fee you would have paid. This is known as fee-based remuneration, which should also be a sign of quality. Fees vary widely, depending on the quality of the adviser and location (advisers in Central London will be more expensive than those in the North of England). On average, fees are £150 an hour, or 1 per cent of your investment portfolio. This probably sounds expensive, but if you were to pay via commission on products sold, you might well end up paying far more over time.

You also need to put the fees in context. Would you be happy to pay a plumber £60 an hour to sort out a problem in your bathroom? If so, surely it's worth paying £150 an hour to ensure financial security and a comfortable retirement?

And finally . . .

Financial decisions can be sensitive and often give rise to strong emotions. Your financial adviser is a person to whom you will have to tell intimate details about your family and its money, so you need to choose someone with whom you have good chemistry. You need to trust your adviser and have confidence in his or her abilities.

For this reason, the Financial Services Authority recommends you shop around for a financial adviser. Contact organisations that can give you a list of advisers in your local area – see contacts below. Even if friends and family recommend an adviser, talk to two or three before making your decision.

Before your first meeting

If you want the best service from a financial adviser, you'll have to do some background preparation before the first meeting. Knowing your financial priorities is essential: there's no point going to an IFA with the vague idea of a need for financial advice. You first need to have a firm idea of the life you wish to lead and your personal financial goals. Identify the specific goals that you plan to save for, such as buying a new car, a deposit on a home, a holiday of a lifetime, sending your children to university, paying off credit card debt, planning for retirement and so on.

Also have a clear picture of the progress you have made to date towards reaching each of these goals. Include how much you have saved, where your money is located and how much money you owe.

Next, you need to think about the timeframe. In an ideal world, how soon would you like to accomplish these goals? Break down each goal into short-term (1 year or less), medium-term (1 to 3 years) or long-term (5 or more years). If you explain all of these details to the adviser, you should get a better service.

QUESTIONS TO ASK AN ADVISER

What experience do you have?

Find out how long they have been in practice and
the different companies with which they have been
associated.

What qualifications do you have?

Qualifications aren't everything – experience is often
just as valuable. However, higher qualifications do
show that the IFA has a certain level of knowledge. You
should also find out what steps the adviser takes to
stay current with changes and developments in the
financial planning field.

What is your approach to financial planning?

Ask the adviser about the type of clients and financial
situations he or she typically likes to work with. Some
have a holistic approach to your finances, while others
may specialise in advising on specific areas – mortgages,
for example – or certain types of clients (doctors and
dentists, say).

Will you be the only person working with me?

Advisers may work with you personally or have other
people on hand in or outside the office to assist them.

You may want to meet everyone who will be working with you. If the adviser works with professionals outside his or her own practice to carry out financial recommendations, such as lawyers or accountants, ask for their names so you can check on their backgrounds.

When and where will meetings take place?

Some advisers expect clients to go to their office during working hours for meetings. Others are more flexible, offering evening appointments and home visits. If it's hard to escape from your own workplace during the day, the option of evening or home meetings could be a valuable one.

Could you show me some references from satisfied clients?

Whether it's a financial adviser or a plumber, personal recommendation is always a great start – but if you don't have that, it's good to be able to see that other clients have received sound advice.

What happens if you leave the firm or retire?

Your relationship with your financial adviser will be an ongoing one, renewed as your circumstances change. If your adviser is part of a small company and is approaching retirement, you'll need to know who will step into his or her shoes. With larger firms, where staff turnover may be more of an issue, it's worth clarifying how client handovers are handled.

Be your own financial adviser

If you're confident and knowledgeable about money matters, you'll be able to manage your own financial affairs and investments, just using the guiding hand of a professional in any instances where your own knowledge falls short.

Reading books like this one is a good start in building up your financial knowledge. There are also several financial magazines to turn to and most newspapers run regular money sections, which keep you updated on the fast-moving financial sector. Plus, of course, there's a vast amount of information on the Internet. Not all of this is reliable, however, so make sure you use trusted websites, such as:

- www.moneymadeclear.fsa.gov.uk
- www.thepensionservice.gov.uk
- www.pensionsadvisoryservice.org.uk

Background reading on financial matters and doing your own investment research will help you identify those professional advisers who are likely to be reliable and monitor the quality of advice you receive.

Useful contacts

- The online 'find an IFA service' at **IFA Promotion** (www.unbiased.co.uk, 0800 085 3250) will provide the names and addresses of four independent financial advisers in your local area.
- The **Institute of Financial Planning** (www.financialplanning.org.uk, 0117 945 2470) has a national register of fee-based financial planners.
- **My Local Adviser** (www.mylocaladviser.co.uk) enables you to identify and locate financial advisers in your area.
- The **Personal Finance Society** (www.thepfs.org/findanadviser) can help you find advisers in your local area who have passed at least three financial planning examinations.
- The **Association of Private Client Investment Managers and Stockbrokers** (www.apcims.co.uk, 020 7247 7080) provides a directory of its member stockbrokers and investment managers.
- The **Association of Solicitor Investment Managers** (www.asim.org.uk, 01732 783 548) provides a directory of solicitors who give legal and investment advice.
- The **Financial Services Authority**'s consumer helpline (0845 606 1234) allows you to check that the firms you contact are authorised.

My property is my pension

Money may be a taboo subject for many of us in the UK, but property is one of the most popular dinner-party conversation topics. 'My property is my pension' is a common saying among homeowners, and investing in property is a very popular way of preparing for retirement. The bricks-and-mortar appeal is that you own something solid that you can see and touch. Shares in companies often seem too intangible, but the value of property is easy to understand.

A staggering one-third of British people expect property to provide their retirement income, according to research by insurer AXA. And almost half of savers – 47 per cent – would put their pension savings into residential property, according to research by Alexander Forbes Financial Services.

Anyone who bought property in the late 1990s has done phenomenally well out of the investment. According to figures from the Halifax, average house prices have risen by nearly *200* per cent over the past 10 years. Against this background, a buy-to-let property may seem the ideal investment for retirement: you could benefit from capital growth and you'll also receive a rental income – some investors see this income as their pension when they reach retirement.

In principle, buy-to-let can be a very attractive pension alternative. A relatively small lump sum can be geared up into a large investment using mortgage borrowing. During the years to retirement, it's reasonable to expect that property management, maintenance and mortgage repayments will be covered by the rental income. Then, if all goes well, at retirement the mortgage will be paid off and the future rent will provide a useful monthly cash flow to use as retirement income.

When you retire, if you need a lump sum, you could sell the property, though you'll have to pay capital gains tax (CGT) on the profit. Alternatively, you could hold on to the property and pass it on to your children, taking expert advice to minimise inheritance tax liabilities. One of the big complaints about conventional pensions is that they can't be passed on to future generations.

But most independent financial advisers will recommend that you tread carefully when it comes to buy-to-let investments for the following reasons:

■ property is illiquid and inflexible – you can't convert property into cash quickly, or get your money out at short notice or in small amounts;

- property isn't tax-efficient, as you'll have to pay income tax on the rent and CGT when you sell;
- property isn't always easy to manage – tenants can be problematic and will contact you at all hours to sort out plumbing problems and so on. If you employ an agent to make life easier, you'll reduce your rental income;
- rental income from property varies according to market conditions and may not be the most profitable source of income. There are often better ways to invest.

If you do go ahead, proceed with caution and with realistic expectations.

Plan to own a property for at least 10 years. The costs of property acquisition and sale are considerable, so it's a real mistake to dip in and out of the market. Stamp duty alone adds 1 per cent to the purchase price of properties between £60,000 and £250,000, and 3 per cent between £250,000 and £500,000. Remember, too, that location is crucial, so do your research on the area you have in mind.

Before you do anything, make sure the figures add up for a worst-case scenario. For instance, would you be able to cope for several months without a tenant when you have to cover the mortgage, or a rise in interest rates? And budget for a slush fund to keep the property well maintained.

Be fully aware that 'My property is my pension' is a risky strategy. Placing all your eggs in one basket in this manner really does leave you overly exposed to house-price movements. Your pension should be invested in diversified assets – not just property – that are in line with your age, lifestyle commitments and the number of years before you'll reach retirement.

Rent a room for extra cash

Many property-owners raise extra income by renting out a room in their home. This could be a good way to raise the money you need to start a retirement fund. It could also help fund your son or daughter's university tuition fees, and could even generate income in retirement.

Of course, you need a spare room to make this work! And you need to be comfortable sharing your house with a stranger. But that person may not have to be a stranger – you may find a family member or friend who needs somewhere to live. And your lodger may not need to live with you for the whole year – if you live in a university town, why not let to students in term time? Or perhaps you could do a summer-school let?

Here's the key advantage of letting a room in your home – it can bring you up to £4,250 a year (around £350 a month) tax-free income. Rental income is normally subject to tax. However, if you're letting part of your home, you're exempt from tax on the first £4,250. This is due to a government scheme called 'Rent a Room' designed to encourage people to take in lodgers. If you're a mortgage payer, it's best to check whether taking in a lodger is within your mortgage lender's and insurer's terms and conditions before advertising the room.

How 'Rent a Room' works

You let out a furnished room or part of your main home – it can be a whole floor. It must be furnished, as unfurnished rooms don't qualify for the scheme. Also note that the scheme doesn't apply if your home is converted into separate flats that you rent out. In this case you'll need to declare your rental income to HM Revenue & Customs (HMRC) and pay tax in the normal way.

You don't have to be a homeowner. If you have your landlord's consent you can take advantage of the scheme as a tenant. If you don't normally fill out a tax return and the income is below £4,250, you don't have to do anything – the exemption is automatic. If the amount you earn is above that figure, just let your tax office know.

If you usually fill out a self-assessment tax return, consider whether you're better off in the scheme or not. Under the scheme you can't claim expenses for wear and tear, insurance etc. so it may not be ideal for your circumstances. If you spend more on decorating a room and keeping it in order than you're getting for it, you'll be making a loss.

Allowable expenses when letting a room if you are opting out of the Rent a Room scheme include:

- letting agent's fees
- legal fees for lets of a year or less, or for renewing a lease for less than 50 years
- accountants' fees
- buildings and contents insurance
- interest on property loans
- maintenance and repairs (but not improvements)
- utility bills
- rent, ground rent, service charges
- council tax
- services you pay for, e.g. cleaning
- direct costs of letting the property, e.g. phone calls, stationery and advertising

Equity release

There's also another way in which your home can be your pension provider. Unless you are very unlucky, rising property prices and inflation mean your property will be worth more at your retirement than it was when you bought it.

The value of your property, excluding any outstanding mortgage, is called 'equity'. An equity-release scheme simply allows you to access some of this equity to spend as you wish, while continuing to live in the property. Once you are 55 or older and own your own home (or have a very small mortgage), you may be able to generate a cash lump sum or a regular income by using an equity-release scheme. This can dramatically enhance your lifestyle in retirement, but it must be considered very carefully because there are many downsides.

Equity release is probably the last major financial decision anyone makes in his or her lifetime. It's definitely an area in which you should take financial and legal advice before signing up, so you're fully aware of both the process and the alternatives before jumping in.

In October 2007, the demand for equity release was up 10 per cent on the previous year, while the amount of equity released from UK homes was up by 26 per cent, having broken the £1 billion barrier. These figures are expected to keep on rising as more and more people see their home as their biggest asset to help fund their retirement.

By far the best way to release the equity in your home is to sell up and move to a cheaper property – swap your four-bedroom house for a two-bed flat. However, this isn't an option for everyone. Many people don't realise how emotionally attached they can become to a family home. If you've lived in the area for many years, downsizing is bound to be a huge upheaval. In fact, you simply may not feel able to leave a home that evokes many memories and has sentimental attachments for you. Similarly, you may not be able to face moving away from friends and family, or having to change doctor (this can be a very important issue for anyone in later life who is suffering ill health).

By the time they retire, people are often loath to 'rob their children of their inheritance' by handing over their home to an equity-release company. This can scupper plans to take an income from the equity in their home. However, you may find that when you reach retirement, your children encourage you to live life to the full rather than struggle on so that you can leave them the family home as an inheritance. Not all children will feel this way, however. And you may find that your children are in a position to help *you* out financially, which can sometimes work out better for them than if you raise funds through equity release.

Nevertheless, spending the kids' inheritance (or 'SKI-ing') is becoming an increasingly popular trend, as more and more people choose, or are compelled, to tap into the equity in their homes to finance their retirement, leaving less for the next generation.

Equity release basics

There's no tax to pay on a cash lump sum that you raise through an equity-release scheme. However, if you invest the money raised, you could be liable to tax on the interest from a savings account or returns from an investment scheme. If you opt for a plan that provides an income, part of that income may be subject to tax, depending on your financial circumstances.

There are two types of equity-release product.

Lifetime mortgages are the most popular product. These allow you to release a percentage of the value of the property with a loan that is secured against the value of the property. Homeowners receive a cash lump sum and aren't required to make any interest payments during the term of the loan. Instead, interest is 'rolled up' and is repaid in addition to the loan from the final sale of the property when you die or if you have to enter long-term residential care.

Interest rates on lifetime mortgages are higher than on conventional mortgages because the lender is taking on additional risk. First, there's the risk that property prices might not rise at a rate sufficient to cover the roll-up of interest (this becomes more likely the longer the borrower lives). The lender also faces an interest-rate risk. Lifetime mortgages differ from conventional mortgages in that the interest rate is fixed for the life of the customer.

One of the key advantages of lifetime mortgages is that you continue to own your property and therefore benefit from any rises in property prices. Obviously you'll need to understand exactly what you're taking on with a lifetime mortgage. Ask the provider for an illustration of what your repayments will be if you live 10 years beyond your average life expectancy. This will allow you to consider the potential impact of the scheme on any inheritance you may wish to leave.

Reversion plans are the less popular alternative to lifetime mortgages. If you're releasing equity in your 50s or 60s, rather than in your 70s and 80s, you might be able to release more cash through a reversion plan than you could get with a lifetime mortgage. However, people tend not to like them as much because these plans involve selling a share in your property as opposed to borrowing money against it.

The way reversion plans work is as follows. A percentage of the homeowner's property is sold to the reversion company in exchange for a cash lump sum. The homeowner retains a lifetime tenancy and the freedom to move home whenever he or she chooses. Both parties share in any increase in value of the property. When the homeowner or their surviving spouse dies, the property is sold and any gain is divided according to the percentage of the property owned.

If you do a full reversion – effectively selling your whole property – you won't benefit from rises in property prices and won't leave an inheritance for your family.

Safe Home Income Plans

Make sure that the equity-release company is a member of SHIP (Safe Home Income Plans). Equity-release schemes supplied by members of the group offer a 'no negative equity' guarantee, which promises consumers that they will never owe more than the value of their home. Also, all SHIP providers guarantee consumers a right of tenure for life as well as the freedom to move home in the future without penalty. For more information visit www.ship-ltd.org or telephone them on 0870 241 60 60.

Take independent advice

Retired homeowners in the UK are paying significantly over the odds on equity-release deals by going direct to a product provider rather than an independent adviser, according to research in 2007 by Key Retirement Solutions, an independent equity-release adviser. Many consumers believe that by cutting out an adviser they'll save money on fees, but when it comes to equity release, this isn't typically the case. In fact, some of the big lifetime-mortgage lenders charge customers a higher interest rate if they go direct to them rather than going through an adviser for the very same deal. Even if the fee charged for advice is taken into consideration, the savings can still be substantial.

What's more fundamentally important here is that equity release isn't a straightforward commodity product that should be bought solely on price. There are many factors to take into consideration, and equity release isn't suitable for everyone. This is why it's even more important to seek specialist advice. A direct provider certainly won't tell people that they get a better rate if they go through an intermediary.

For a free and independent guide to equity release, go to www.keyrs.co.uk or call Key Retirement Solutions free on 0800 531 6027.

Your mortgage

It's great to own your home for many reasons, both emotional and financial. Paying off your mortgage ahead of schedule can feel great, but this shouldn't interfere with funding your retirement.

It still makes more financial sense to buy rather than rent in the UK – but only just. Research from Abbey Mortgages found that the average monthly cost of a mortgage for 25 years and the average monthly cost of rent for the same period are converging. However, while the cost of renting and buying is converging, this doesn't account for the fact that with a repayment mortgage, you end up owning the property when the 25 years are up. In addition, homeowners benefit from any capital appreciation (assuming that the property increases in value) that might be earned during that period.

By the time you retire, you'll ideally have paid off any mortgage on your home. This isn't possible for everyone, though. Scottish Widows reveals that around one in five (over 1.1 million) retired homeowners in the UK have an outstanding mortgage on their home – with an average debt of £38,000. What's more, one in eight owe more than £50,000, putting increased pressure on retirement income.

Most lenders will let you overpay your mortgage by 10 per cent each year without incurring penalties. This will not only increase the equity in your home but also reduce the length of your loan. For example, overpaying a 25-year £100,000 mortgage at 6 per cent by £64 a month will cut the length of the mortgage by over four years. It will also slash your interest bill by almost £20,000.

The psychological freedom of not having a mortgage is very appealing, but the argument for trying to invest the extra cash at a higher rate is compelling too. Normally, you should only pay off your mortgage early if the interest rate is higher than the return you might expect to get by investing your money instead. If your mortgage rate is low, say 5 per cent, you're probably better off investing the extra each month. For example, if you repay your home loan ahead of schedule, you're basically earning a 5 per cent return, which represents the amount of interest you avoided paying by making the extra payments. However, you should be able to do better than that over the long term by investing in a diversified portfolio of shares, albeit with greater risk to your capital.

But this isn't only a financial issue; there's an emotional and psychological dimension to this decision. If the idea of owning your home outright without a mortgage really appeals to you and will make you enjoy life more, devoting at least some money to prepaying your mortgage makes sense. It's especially sensible if you're timing the pay-off so you enter retirement without a mortgage payment hanging over your head. That said, it's not sensible to let the warm feeling you get from paying down your mortgage to disadvantage you financially. So before you devote resources to early payment of a mortgage, make sure that you've started building a decent nest egg, for example by contributing enough to an employer-sponsored pension to get the employer's contribution.

ARGUMENTS IN FAVOUR OF OVERPAYING THE MORTGAGE

- You want to have more options and choices in life, and eliminating your mortgage debt frees you up to achieve this.
- You want a guaranteed rate of return and can ensure such a savings rate only if you pay off your mortgage. Investing means putting money in a financial product that involves taking a risk – in the hope that the money will grow more quickly – but it could lose value. A top-performing investment will pay more than 10 per cent a year, but one that performs badly can lose serious amounts of money.
- By showing a willingness to boost the equity in your home, you put yourself in a better position to access better-value products.
- You want to buy a bigger home in a couple of years.
- You can pay off your 30-year mortgage quickly, say in 5 years. You will skip 25 years of interest payments, saving a huge amount of money.
- The amount you've invested is greater than the balance of the mortgage. You're not overly invested in residential property. If your assets are stock-heavy, it may be a good idea to throw more at your mortgage.

- You want to manage risk. Paying off your mortgage is a form of insurance against losing your job and income, interest hikes, market crashes and banks pulling back their mortgage lines, making it difficult to get a good mortgage deal. It ensures your family will not be homeless. You want to sacrifice potentially higher returns to avoid an unexpected financial disaster.

ARGUMENTS AGAINST OVERPAYING THE MORTGAGE

- A very large number of people with great wealth still carry a mortgage, and the biggest debt that most people have in their lives is the mortgage on their home. It's common to hear people repeat the principle 'always try to be debt-free', but mortgage loans can be viewed as low-interest, manageable debt that enables greater overall acquisition of wealth.
- You are convinced that the money can be better serviced in another investment with better returns.
- Your extra payments will enable you to get rid of your 30-year mortgage in 25 years. Invest them over 25 years and you should do much better.

- Maximising contributions to a pension means you're taking advantage of 'free money' – the upfront tax relief, plus perhaps the matching contribution from your employer.
- By repaying your mortgage, you're not altering the state of your investment in property – your house is neither more nor less likely to rise or fall in value.
- Money thrown at the mortgage is trapped, and in many cases you can't get to it without paying a fee. You can liquidate an investment portfolio easily to smooth over rough financial spots in your life, but you can't feed your family with the equity in your home.

Things to put in place before saving for retirement

What would you do if you lost your job? Could your family survive? And if so, for how long? Do you want to risk losing your house through defaulting on your mortgage repayments? What would you do if you had an expensive family emergency? Imagine your teenage daughter is on a round-the-world trip and falls off a moped in Thailand, resulting in a trip to hospital. She has no travel insurance and you have to fly her back home at great expense. Or how would you manage if the car and the washing machine needed major repairs in the same month?

Establishing an emergency cash fund

There are many reasons why you should build an emergency cash fund and make it your financial priority. First of all, it will keep you afloat if something unexpected crops up. Financial advisers recommend that you put aside at least 3 months' – preferably 6 months' – salary in an easy-access cash account. If you have many financial dependants, you may only feel comfortable with a larger emergency cash fund – perhaps the equivalent of a year's salary. However, make sure that the money in your cash fund is working as hard as it can. Many bank and building society accounts pay rubbish rates of interest. You need to find one that pays more than the current rate of inflation, otherwise your money is losing its value.

Cash accounts usually deduct 20 per cent of the interest as savings tax. So if your account pays 5 per cent interest, you'll only receive 4 per cent. And if inflation is 3 per cent, your deposit is only really growing at 1 per cent a year.

Your best option is to put as much of your emergency cash fund as possible into a cash ISA where it will probably get a top rate of interest, plus avoid the 20 per cent savings tax. Not all cash ISAs are easily accessible, though, so before you choose a particular cash ISA as a home for your emergency fund, check how long it will take to access your money.

You can only put £3,600 a year into a cash ISA, so it may take a few years to transfer all your emergency fund into ISAs. Couples have double the allowance though, so you may want to put some of your funds in a cash ISA for your partner. In the meantime, you can keep the surplus monies in a normal bank or building society account, but make sure you're getting a decent rate.

Get the right financial protection

Bonnie Burns, product marketing director at Legal & General, has summed up the general attitude towards financial protection: 'The nation's priorities seem misguided, with people more worried about losing their mobile than about how they would cope financially if they had a critical illness. We all know that it is difficult to face up to our own mortality, but when insuring possessions is prioritised above insuring lives, then something has to be done. Protection insurance is widely available, value-for-money and easy to arrange, so there's no reason not to consider it.'

Income-protection insurance: the cinderella of insurance policies

Protecting your income is more important than saving for retirement because if you haven't got an income, you won't be able to build up a pension pot. This is where insurance comes into play, particularly income-protection insurance, though you may also need life insurance and critical-illness insurance, depending on your circumstances.

The last thing that many people insure is the one thing that pays for everything else – their income, in other words. But it's madness not to protect yourself and your family by taking out income-protection insurance, which will give you a regular tax-free income if you're injured or too ill to work. It's the best-kept secret of the financial services industry, and you may not have heard of this type of insurance as it's not nearly as well promoted as life insurance or its ugly sister, payment-protection insurance. However, the average man under 50 is twice as likely to be off work for more than six months because of an accident or sickness than he is to die. Also, bear in mind that if you're seriously disabled, your living costs are likely to rise to allow you to cope with your disability.

Even if you have a family and children, income protection is often viewed as more important than life insurance. Think through the impact of your death compared to illness or disability: if you die your family will miss your income. However, if you're seriously ill or disabled, your family not only loses your income but also has to find extra money to support you. In blunt terms, you're a more expensive liability to your family if you're injured or seriously ill than if you die.

It's important to get the right type of income protection and not confuse real income protection with the inferior payment-protection insurance, which is usually sold alongside loans, mortgages and credit cards. This latter type of policy will only pay out an income for a maximum of one to two years, and often has clauses in the policy that enable it to refuse to pay out in some circumstances, perhaps for stress-related illnesses, for example. It does, however, have its place if you can't get income protection because of poor health – payment protection doesn't require medical underwriting.

A genuine income-protection policy is sometimes known as 'permanent health insurance' and continues to pay out until you are either well enough to return to work, you reach retirement age, or (worst-case scenario!) you die – depending on which happens first.

What you need to know about income protection

- An income-protection policy is fully underwritten, which means you'll be asked numerous personal questions on application. The price you pay will depend on your age, sex, general health (including whether you smoke) and employment status. Those in professional, office-based jobs generally pay less than those in physically demanding jobs.
- It's best to take out an 'own occupation' policy, so that if you can't do your current job you can claim. Some policies are written on inferior 'any occupation' terms, which means you would be forced to take up other perhaps less desirable or lower-status employment if your health permitted.

- A full income-protection policy is sometimes known as permanent health insurance.

- Income protection is generally more expensive than payment protection, but you are getting a far superior and much better-value policy. If you want to cut the price of income protection, you can lengthen the time period after which the policy starts to pay out. Some policies pay out as soon as you become ill or suffer a disability, but you could change this to a year or two years after you become seriously ill or disabled. You need to ensure you have enough savings to last until the policy pays out.

- The maximum monthly benefit is usually a tax-free payment equal to around 65 per cent of your gross income.

- Policy wordings differ and there are important rules and conditions attached to policies. For this reason, it's very important that you seek independent financial advice before taking out income-protection insurance.

Important note for employees

Before taking out a policy, check whether your employer already covers you. If you work for a large organisation, it's very likely that your employer provides you with some form of income protection through the company insurance scheme. You need to check what level of cover is provided, though, as many company schemes only pay out for six months. If this is the case, you'll need to top up your protection with private insurance.

THINGS TO PUT IN PLACE BEFORE SAVING FOR RETIREMENT

NUMBER CRUNCHING

- You are 26 times more likely to be incapacitated and off work for more than six months than you are to die before the age of 65 (source: Norwich Union).
- Only 9 per cent of workers have an income-protection policy sufficient to cover their outgoings, should they lose their income (source: Alliance & Leicester).

What you get from the state

Some people are happy to rely on the state, and for them income protection isn't suitable. However, they may not realise that state help is very thin on the ground: there's no state help with mortgage payments, for example. People who can't work as a result of illness or disability may be able to receive incapacity benefit, a weekly payment for people under the state pension age. For the first 28 weeks off work, you could be eligible for £63.75 a week. For weeks 29 to 52, the payment rises to £75.40. The long-term rate paid for absences over 53 weeks is £84.50 (2008/09 figures).

Other benefits may include housing benefit or a reduction in council tax. However, for anyone with a family to support or a mortgage to pay, these won't stretch far.

Do you need life insurance?

Many people make the mistake of taking out life insurance to protect their mortgage when they don't need it. If you don't have financial dependants, life insurance isn't necessary and you'll be much better off with an income protection policy.

Life insurance pays a lump sum if you die during the term of the policy. Critical-illness cover pays a lump sum if you're diagnosed with a life-threatening condition such as cancer or heart disease. (Life and critical illness are sometimes combined in the same policy.) With both types of insurance, premiums increase as you get older and you'll pay more if you have health problems that reduce your life expectancy.

Family-income benefit

This is often the most cost-effective type of family protection. Rather than providing a lump sum should you die, family-income benefit provides a regular, tax-free, monthly income for you and your dependants – from the time of the claim to the end of the plan term.

For example, if the plan term is 20 years and the claim is made after 16 years, benefits will be paid for the remaining 4 years. This is why family-income benefit often costs less than life insurance. Family-income benefit is particularly attractive to those who like to know they have a regular monthly income and would rather not have to worry about complex investment decisions to make the most of a lump sum pay-out.

The importance of making a will

Everyone should make a will. But not many people do. In fact, only one in three people in the UK have a will prepared (according to research from Barclays Wealth). However, wills are one of the easiest ways to protect your wealth and the only way to be sure that your wishes are fulfilled. They also avoid any misunderstandings.

FOUR GOOD REASONS TO MAKE A WILL

1 *You* decide who benefits. Without a will, the law decides who benefits. Therefore, if you fail to make a will, the people to whom you'd like to leave your estate may receive little, or nothing at all, and others to whom you wanted to leave nothing may end up benefiting.

2 You can appoint guardians for your children. Terrible accidents do occur, and responsible parents should consider what would happen to their children if they weren't there. It's possible to appoint guardians who'll be responsible for your

children's upbringing if neither parent is alive. You can also appoint someone you trust to look after your assets until the children are old enough to take responsibility for themselves.

3 **You can make sure your partner inherits.** Unmarried partners and partners who have not registered a civil partnership cannot inherit from each other unless there is a will.

4 **Your beneficiaries may incur less inheritance tax.** It may be possible to reduce the amount of tax payable on a large inheritance if advice is taken in advance and a will is made.

Dying without a will

If you die without making a will, you die 'intestate' and your estate will be distributed according to the law of intestacy. It doesn't matter what you may have wished for or promised while you were alive: the law decides who gets what.

The intestacy rules could leave your family struggling to survive financially. They could also mean that your wealth is passed to family members that you might not have wanted to be included. Friends get nothing under the laws of intestacy and, again, this may be something you're not happy about. If you have no will, it surprises many people to find out that your husband or wife won't automatically inherit all your estate.

Here's what happens under the law in England and Wales (there are different laws in Scotland and Ireland, see below) if you are:

- **Married with children.** By law, a surviving spouse receives the chattels (your goods and personal belongings), the first £125,000 and a life interest in half of the rest. The children receive the other half of the residue in equal shares.

- **Married without children.** Your spouse gets the first £200,000, plus half the balance. The remaining half goes to your other relatives in this order of priority: parents, brothers/sisters, half brothers/sisters, grandparents, aunts/uncles.

- **Unmarried, with children.** Your estate will be shared equally between the children. Should they die before you then their children (your grandchildren) would take the share that would have gone to them.

- **Unmarried, without children, but with relatives.** Your estate will be shared among relatives in this order of priority: parents, brothers/sisters (or their children if they died while the deceased was still alive), half brothers/sisters, grandparents, aunts/uncles (or their children if they died while the deceased was still alive), half uncles or aunts (or their children if they died while the deceased was still alive).

- **Unmarried and without relatives.** Your whole estate goes to the Crown.

The law on intestacy does not recognise a 'common law' wife or husband but it does recognise a civil partner. If you aren't legally married, you get nothing, although if you can prove that you were financially dependent on the deceased, you may be able to apply for provision from the estate. However, this can be expensive and time-consuming, and may not necessarily be successful. If a divorce is finalised before the death, the marriage is over and the former wife or husband gets nothing. Except for spouses, only blood relatives inherit. If, for instance, a brother would have inherited a share but died first, his widow will not get his share (although his children will).

How to make a will

Drawing up a will is very straightforward these days, particularly with the help of computers and the Internet. A solicitor may charge you as little as £100 for a straightforward will, and if you and your partner create identical wills (called 'mirror wills') you're likely to get a reduced rate for the two. A solicitor will usually store your will for you without charge, though you don't have to use a solicitor, and a will can be perfectly valid without being drawn up or witnessed by one.

An alternative option is to write your own will, perhaps with the aid of a will-writing kit, which you can buy from supermarkets, stationers or online. However, only consider a DIY will if your affairs are straightforward. The DIY approach leaves you open to making a mistake, and if this should happen, then you've only yourself to blame. You could also go to a will writer, who's not a qualified lawyer but will still charge you for making a will. If you do, then check the firm's credentials thoroughly.

You can find further information on intestacy and making a will in England and Wales at www.direct.gov.uk. If you live in Scotland, go to www.scotland.gov.uk; residents of Northern Ireland can find information at www.northernireland.gov.uk.

Introduction to investing

There's no perfect investment – otherwise we'd all be rich! If you want your money to be safe, it's unlikely that you'll ever get a great return. On the other hand, if you're prepared to take some risk, your money could double or triple overnight – or you could lose the lot by the morning. You have to balance risk and reward – and it makes sense only to take risks that you feel comfortable with.

Learning how to invest is a daunting task for most people because it means you have to become familiar with certain aspects of the stock market. But if you take the task seriously, a little knowledge can go a long way.

You can't separate out investing from your own personal goals – they're inextricably linked. Your individual financial aims will dictate how you invest. And you'll need to adjust your investments as you go through life. Buying a home, getting married, having children, getting a promotion at work, nearing retirement and stopping work are all events that will affect your investment strategy and goals. You may need a small lump sum at certain times, a large lump sum for other events, and once you reach retirement you'll need to generate an income from your investments.

When you're in your 40s, you're most likely to be a growth investor. This means you're putting aside money on a regular basis for the long term and hoping that this 'capital' will grow. However, you may also have some short-term goals, or you may need to generate an income from your investments. And at some point you may have a windfall in the form of an inheritance or bonus.

The difference between saving and investing

Saving and investing are both things that we do with our spare money, but there are key differences. Saving is a way of giving our day-to-day life some security so that we don't find ourselves short of cash in an emergency. Investing is more about planning for expensive events a few years in the future, like a child's university education or 20 years of retirement.

When you save money in a bank or building society account, you're guaranteed to get back the sum you put in, plus interest. Investing gives you no such guarantee. Your capital (the money you invest at the start) is at risk (you could end up with nothing). In return for taking on this risk, you expect to get a much higher rate of return than a bank or building society account would give.

We've already seen how inflation can make the return on cash accounts look miserable. Residential property has had great returns but is awkward to manage and, after 10 years of fantastic growth, prospects are looking uncertain.

If you're investing for the long term – more than five years – experts agree that you should be putting most if not all of your money in shares, also called 'equities'. Buying shares means investing in companies like British Airways, Shell, Marks & Spencer, Tesco, Vodafone, United Utilities and Unilever, plus other smaller companies that are not such well-known household names.

Lots of studies have shown that over the years, shares produce the best returns of all the different asset classes. One of the best known and most respected studies is the Barclays Capital Equity Gilt Study. This shows that UK equities have returned on average a real return (above inflation) of 7.2 per cent a year over the last 50 years. In contrast, cash has returned just 2 per cent above inflation a year.

Note that these figures show what shares have produced in the past, and there's no guarantee that shares will continue to perform in this way – however, this is the best way to estimate what they might produce in future.

Shares will have good years and bad years, good months and bad months. This is why you need to invest for the long term, to smooth out the bumps in performance, putting money aside in shares for at least five years – preferably a decade. And this money must be cash that you can afford to lose: in other words, that you could survive without in your day-to-day life.

If you're going to invest directly in shares, you'll need to dedicate lots of time and effort to successful stock picking. Most people don't have this sort of time and therefore prefer to invest in collective investment vehicles described in Chapter 10. However, if you want to take the DIY approach to investing in shares, you'll have to read some books about stock picking and investment strategies, and if you *really* want to get ahead in the stock market, then becoming familiar with accounting is a necessity.

The power of compounding

To Albert Einstein, compound interest was the eighth wonder of the world. He's quoted as saying: 'The most powerful force in the universe is compound interest'.

When it comes to investing, compounding means that you earn interest on your initial investment, as well as on any other interest you may have accumulated. So if you earn 5 per cent on £100, after a year you'll have £105. After two years, you'll have not £110, but £110.25. After 20 years, you'll have not £200, but £265.

Another important fact about compounding is that a small increase in the rate of return can produce a big impact over time. If you up the rate of interest to 7 per cent on your

£100, after 20 years you'll have £380, i.e. £115 more than if you'd got a 5 per cent return.

So if you're offered two investments that aim to bring 7 per cent, but one charges 1.5 per cent to manage the investment and the other charges 0.5 per cent, obviously go for the cheapest. That 1 per cent difference in charges can make all the difference to the end result.

The benefits of saving early in life are greatly magnified by compounding, and as time passes, the power of compounding accelerates dramatically. The good news is that if you're 40, you still have time on your side. Getting started with investing as early as possible can make a big difference to how much wealth is ultimately accumulated. So don't delay, start today.

The Rule of 72

If you want to do simple compound interest problems in your head, the 'Rule of 72' gives you a lightning-fast benchmark to determine how good (or not so good) a potential investment is likely to be. The rule of 72 says that in order to find the number of years required to double your money at a given interest rate, all you have to do is divide the interest rate into 72.

For example, if you want to know how long it will take to double your money at 7 per cent interest, divide 7 into 72 and get 10 years. Or if you want to double your money in six years, just divide 6 into 72 to find that it will require an interest rate of about 12 per cent.

The rule of 72 is remarkably accurate, as long as the interest rate is less than 20 per cent.

Lump sum or regular savings?

Many investors invest lump sums, for example into an ISA or a pension, either at the end of the tax year (when they know how much extra they can save) or when they think they'll benefit from stock-market conditions.

Lump sums aren't necessarily the best strategy, however, as the odds for getting market-timing decisions right are terrible. A better option is to commit money to an investment plan on a regular and consistent basis. Regular savings plans remove the need to make market-timing decisions and also enable you to benefit from what is known as 'pound-cost averaging'.

When you invest a fixed cash amount each month, you automatically buy more units or shares when the stock market falls and prices are low, and fewer units when prices are high. Because you automatically buy more units when prices fall, the average cost of units you buy will be lower than the actual average price over the same period.

In a year when the market fluctuates around its starting point, ending up with very little increase, a regular savings plan could beat the same money invested as a lump sum at the start of the year. The more erratic the price performance of a fund, the greater the positive effects of pound-cost averaging.

The two enemies of investors: inflation and tax

If you're looking to the long term, anything that's going to eat into your investment returns is a problem. That's why the two biggest enemies of investors are inflation and tax. Unfortunately, you can't avoid the effects of inflation eroding your savings and investments, but there are plenty of things you can do to reduce the amount of tax you pay.

Inflation

Inflation is relatively low these days but it can still have a powerful effect on your savings. This is why you shouldn't put your money under the mattress – you have to make it grow.

Money languishing in bank accounts that pay less than 1 per cent interest is losing its value on a daily basis. That's fine, you say. I have my money in an account that pays

5 per cent, so I'm doing really well. Sadly, not the case! If you're a taxpayer, you're paying 20 per cent tax on your savings. So you're actually getting a return of 4 per cent on your money.

Let's say it has to earn at least 3 per cent to beat the annual increase in the cost of everyday living. The first 3 per cent of the return enables your money to hold its value. So you're only getting a 'real return' of 1 per cent. Now that headline rate of 5 per cent return doesn't seem so great. Over 10 years at 1 per cent, £100 invested would only grow to £110.46. Not good.

And with studies showing that many people feel actual inflation is far higher than the government's figures, the cost of living could be rising at a much faster pace than the government would have us believe. If this is true then it becomes even more important never to forget about inflation and to consider investments that will beat this hidden enemy.

Tax

As Benjamin Franklin said so famously, 'In this world nothing is certain but death and taxes'. Yes, tax is inevitable and unavoidable. It's everywhere and affects everyone in countless ways – whether they're individuals, employees or business owners.

Taxation is also complicated and confusing and therefore widely misunderstood. Amazingly, half of those surveyed by accountants PricewaterhouseCoopers mistakenly believe that prescription charges and passport fees are taxes. And despite 31 million (70 per cent) of UK adults claiming to resent rising tax bills, over three quarters (78 per cent) admit to doing nothing to help reduce the amount they pay, according to research from IFA Promotion.

An important key to getting your finances organised is to appreciate how tax reduces your income. From your income you're going to make savings, so if you can pay less tax, you can make greater savings. I need to emphasise here that I'm concerned with legitimate ways to help you reduce your tax bill – tax avoidance rather than tax evasion!

You also need to understand that your investments will be subject to tax. Putting your money in tax-efficient investments is a good idea because it will increase the amount you get back at the end of the investment period.

To tax experts, 1 June is known as Tax Freedom Day, and marks the theoretical point in the year at which we stop working for the government and start working for ourselves. The average British taxpayer spends the first 151 days of the year working to earn enough to pay off their tax burden to the government. So that's five months' work to pay tax bills, and only seven months of the year earning money for ourselves.

It's disheartening to think that for nearly half of the year we're working simply to pay our tax bill, which is why it's so important that you make your hard-earned cash work for you. If you're willing to spend a few spare hours getting your finances in order, rather than paying unnecessary money to the taxman, then you'll be reaping substantial rewards in the long term.

There are many what are called 'tax-efficient' savings and investment products that can give your savings and investments a boost. However, there's a common saying among financial experts: 'Don't let the tax tail wag the investment dog'. In other words, it's not wise to invest in a product simply for its tax advantages. Unfortunately, there are numerous bad 'tax-efficient' savings and investment products. If a product is going to pay a mediocre interest rate, or give poor investment growth, then the money you lose will override the tax advantage compared to other better-performing savings and investment products.

There are many reasons why you could be paying more tax than you need to, but with an understanding of the taxes most likely to affect your finances, and some simple planning, you should be able to reduce your tax bill.

Income tax

Do you really understand how your income is taxed? If you fill out a self-assessment form, you're more likely to understand. However, if you're paid through PAYE (Pay As You Earn), then you may not have given it a thought until now.

In the tax year 2008/09, the first £5,435 of your earned income is free of tax. The next £36,000 slice is taxed at the basic rate of 20 per cent. Earnings over a certain amount – £41,435 in 2008/09 – are taxed at 40 per cent.

If you're a higher-rate taxpayer, this has all sorts of implications for saving and investing.

You can pay less tax by making the best use of your tax-free personal allowances. This is particularly relevant if you're married or in a civil partnership and you and your spouse or partner pay different rates of tax. If, for example, one of you is a higher-rate taxpayer and the other is a basic-rate or non-taxpayer, you can cut your tax liability in half by transferring income-yielding assets like building society deposits or shares to the lower earner.

National Insurance (NI)

National Insurance isn't technically a tax, but it still reduces your income so it's included in this section. (In a survey of over 1,000 people conducted by market researchers TNS on behalf of PricewaterhouseCoopers LLP, three quarters of those surveyed believe that National Insurance contributions (NICs) are a tax.)

It's possible to reduce your NICs using 'salary sacrifice', an arrangement between an employer and employee where the employee agrees to a reduction in salary or bonus, in exchange for a non-cash benefit provided by the employer. For example, this benefit could be a payment to the employee's pension scheme or childcare. And crucially, by reducing the salary or bonus, both employee and employer save on NI.

The employee benefits because he or she can get a higher level of pension payment without a reduction in take-home pay. (As an alternative, the original level of pension payment can be made and the employee can have an increase in take-home pay.) The employer benefits because they'll be paying reduced NI, and they have the option of paying all or some of the NI saving into the employee's pension arrangement.

As the name suggests, salary is being genuinely sacrificed, so any benefits that are based on salary (mortgage or credit card, perhaps) may be affected. In addition, some state benefits are linked to earnings so may also be affected.

Capital Gains Tax (CGT)

This is the other big tax that affects investors. You have capital gains if you invest money, it grows and then you cash it in for a profit. The profit is potentially liable to tax.

In 2008/09, the individual annual exemption is £9,600, so any gains up to this amount within a tax year are free of tax. You should use this allowance efficiently, perhaps by transferring assets between spouses to make the most of both of your CGT allowances: IFA Promotion estimates £510 million a year could be saved in this way.

Inheritance Tax (IHT)

The second most-hated tax after council tax, inheritance tax used to be something that only concerned the very wealthy. But the massive rise in house prices over the past 10 years means many people, particularly those in the South East, are now affected. For more on inheritance tax, turn to Chapter 14.

Tax credits

Find out whether you're eligible for tax credits and claim them: £2.3 billion of 'free money' is up for grabs from HM Revenue & Customs (HMRC) and the Department for Work and Pensions (DWP) in the form of pension credits, child tax credits and working family tax credits. Even reasonably well-off families can be eligible for some help, for example, if both partners are working but the joint income is less than £60,000.

Your tax return

There's no reason to feel inadequate if you feel slightly queasy at the thought of preparing your own tax return. The tax rules are so complicated that many accountants would struggle to calculate their own tax without software to help them. However, the self-assessment tax forms are an annual task that comes around with alarming regularity. But there's no avoiding the job, so you'd better just get on with it and meet the deadline to avoid the £100 fine for late submission.

If you want HMRC to calculate your tax bill, you have to send in your paper tax return by 31 October. After that date, they will still calculate your tax, but won't guarantee to get the calculation to you before the payment date, which is 31 January. Online tax returns can be filed up to 30 December.

Another reason for getting your tax return in before these deadlines is that you can request that any tax underpayments below £2,000 can be collected via your PAYE tax code.

Make sure you sort out your self-assessment within the deadlines: £463 million is unnecessarily paid to HMRC through penalty fines and interest on tax owed. Self-assessment forms received after the 31 January deadline incur penalties of £100; further penalties and errors make up the balance of tax wasted in this way.

Also make sure you fill out the forms correctly. The following two mistakes automatically result in the tax return being rejected:

1 You enter a tick to confirm that you have a particular source of income but the relevant supplementary sheets are not included with the return so it becomes incomplete. Phone the self-assessment orderline on 0845 9000 404 to request any missing supplementary sheets.

2 You forget to sign the return – this is the most common reason for the rejection of a tax return. So after checking your return is complete and accurate, double-check that you've signed and dated it before putting it in the post.

Visit www.taketaxaction.co.uk for tips on how to become more tax-efficient. They also have a useful calculator to help you work out how much tax you're wasting each year.

Your retirement toolkit

When you're planning for a secure retirement, your two best friends will be pensions and individual savings accounts (ISAs). These are 'tax wrappers' into which you can put a range of investments: either ones that are packaged up especially for the purpose by product providers, or ones that you select yourself, if you're feeling confident enough.

Remember, though, that while tax wrappers allow you to reduce the amount of money that ends up in the pocket of HM Revenue & Customs (HMRC), the real key to a secure retirement is the quality and investment performance of the investments you put into the wrappers.

Pensions

Pensions are the obvious choice when saving for retirement. Pension rules dictate that you can't access the money until you're at least 55, so this imposes a useful element of financial discipline on investors. Locking away your savings in a pension removes the temptation to dip into the money for non-retirement purposes. It also means that, on retirement, you'll secure an income for the rest of your life, no matter how long you live or what happens to the stock markets in your old age.

Despite some bad press in recent years, pensions remain the foundation of retirement planning because they have fantastic tax advantages, the likes of which you can't get with any other savings vehicle. For example, you get up-front tax relief on the money you put into a pension. So, for every £100 paid into a pension, a basic-rate taxpayer only has to contribute £80 – the government tops up the balance. Higher-rate taxpayers fork out only £60 for every £100 invested, benefiting from a government top-up of £40.

Money invested in a pension grows free of tax, and then at retirement you can take 25 per cent of the investment as a tax-free lump sum. A downside is that you have to use the remaining 75 per cent of the pension fund to generate an income, and the government has strict rules about how you go about this. It's also difficult after retirement to pass on your pension as an inheritance – there are big tax penalties for people who do this.

Many people who pay higher-rate tax during their working life find that they're basic-rate taxpayers on retirement because they have a lower income than when they were working. You'll need a massive amount invested in a pension to achieve a retirement income around the higher-rate tax level: even a million pound pension pot probably wouldn't get you to the higher-rate tax status in retirement. If you're likely to move from higher to basic-rate taxpayer status in retirement, pensions will work particularly well for you.

However, many people prefer to forego the superior tax advantages of pensions for the greater flexibility that other investments provide. Some people don't like to be told how to invest their money, or when they can access it. Forty year olds may not like the idea of being unable to access the money for 15 years. Others believe that pensions leave you a hostage to fortune because of uncertainty surrounding tax rates and pension regulations far in the future.

If you're put off pensions for whatever reason, there are plenty of other options. What's more, if you decide later on that you'd rather have your money in a pension, the generous pension contributions limits will probably allow you to do so. And you'll still get the upfront tax relief on contributions, whenever you make the switch.

Individual savings accounts (ISAs)

ISAs are a very good alternative to pensions because of their tax treatment, which is almost, but not quite, as good. Although you don't get tax relief up-front on the savings you put into an ISA, your investments grow virtually tax free, as they do in a pension, and when you get to retirement you can take a tax-free income from ISAs, whereas income from a pension will be subject to tax. Basically, with pensions you get the tax benefit on the way in, and with ISAs you get the benefit on the way out.

The key advantage of ISAs becomes clear when you understand how income is taxed in retirement. Pensioners receive a more generous tax-free allowance each year, known as the age-related personal allowance. The government has promised to increase it to £10,000 over the next few years, so couples will receive up to £20,000 of tax-free income in retirement.

A potential problem is that the age allowance is capped by an upper-income limit, and once your total retirement income rises above this level, the government begins to claw back the allowance at the rate of £1 for every £2 above the threshold until it is back in line with the standard personal allowance for non-pensioners.

Importantly, using ISAs to generate a tax-free retirement income doesn't count towards your income limit for age-allowance purposes. This is a great advantage if you're in danger of falling into the 'age allowance trap', whereby you lose your extra personal allowance if your income exceeds a certain limit.

How to generate tax-free retirement income from ISAs

Over the years, you'll hopefully have built up a portfolio of ISAs. Say you started at 40 and invested £6,000 a year in ISAs – that's £500 a month. At retirement aged 65, you'd have a portfolio of the equivalent of £90,000 in today's value if your funds keep pace with inflation. This is a very conservative estimate as you'd expect to do better than inflation. So let's say, again very conservatively, your portfolio has grown to £100,000 – a gain of £10,000.

There are two ways to draw the money from ISAs. The first is as capital gains. You can take up to the current capital gains tax (CGT) limit, which is £9,200 at the time of writing (tax year 2007/08). So in the first year of retirement you might want to go on a round-the-world trip, so you take £9,000 as a capital gain to pay for this. You don't pay any tax on this money.

The second year you need less income, say around £1,800, so you decide to invest your ISA, now worth £91,000, to draw an income. Your ISA is currently fully invested in equities, so you move £60,000 of it into bond funds (see Chapter 9) from which you expect a tax-free income of 3 per cent, i.e. £1,800. The remaining £31,000 you keep invested in equities in the hope of achieving more capital growth.

Investment funds and trusts

If you're one of those people who don't like the rules attached to pension schemes and you have more money to invest than the annual ISA allowance of £7,200, you could invest additional money into investment funds and investment trusts. A good strategy can be to choose funds that focus on 'achieving capital growth' – in other words, growing the sum that you deposited into a bigger sum over time. At retirement you can take the capital growth on your investments and, providing you stick within your annual CGT allowance, you can use these withdrawals as a tax-free income. For more about investment funds and investment trusts, turn to Chapter 10.

National Savings and Investments

National Savings and Investment (NS&I) products are the most secure of all investments because the bank is backed by the government and so can't go bust. Most people should consider holding part of their investment portfolio in National Savings index-linked certificates. These are attractive because your money is safe and your returns are guaranteed to beat inflation. The certificates last three or five years. At the end of the investment term, your investment will have grown in line with the increase in the retail prices index (RPI) and a fixed amount of interest is added on top. Importantly, returns are tax-free. These certificates are therefore particularly beneficial to higher-rate taxpayers.

You can invest between £500 and £15,000 in each issue of index-linked certificates, and there are usually four issues a year.

If you like a gamble, premium bonds may appeal. If you hold the maximum £30,000 in premium bonds and have average luck, you should get regular prizes equal to the prize fund rate (4 per cent tax-free at the time of writing). If you're very lucky, you could win the monthly jackpot of £1 million. However, the odds on winning it are nearly 600,000 to 1. Remember that if your luck runs out, you may not win anything – and your so-called 'investment' could lose its value to inflation over the years.

You can find out more about NS&I by visiting the website www.nsandi.com or phoning 0845 964 5000.

Friendly society tax-free savings

Friendly societies are mutual organisations, owned by their members. They're allowed to offer long-term tax-free savings schemes or investment bonds, up to a maximum contribution limit of £25 a month or £270 a year. The money usually goes into investment funds described as 'with profits'. These invest in a combination of shares, bonds and property. These friendly society bonds aren't subject to income tax and CGT.

Unfortunately, these products often suffer from high charges and mediocre investment performance. They are usually inflexible – you can't access the money easily, as policies tend to be set up for 10 years and there are heavy early-surrender penalties. However, in some circumstances – for example, if you're already fully subscribed to ISAs and don't want to invest in pensions – they can be a useful addition to a portfolio of long-term investments. For further information contact the Association of Friendly Societies at www.afs.org.uk or on 0161 952 5051.

Investment bonds

Investment bonds are sold by life insurance companies. They allow you to invest in a variety of investment funds managed by professional investment managers. They're normally designed to produce long-term capital growth, but can also be used to generate an income. The minimum investment is typically a lump sum of £5,000 or £10,000. When you buy a bond, you'll be allocated a certain number of units in the funds of your choice. Each fund will hold a portfolio of investments, such as shares or bonds, and the price of your units – in other words, the value of your capital – will normally rise and fall in line with the value of these investments. Technically, investment bonds are single-premium life-insurance policies. This means an element of life insurance is provided. But it's tiny, typically adding only an extra 1 per cent or less to the value of your investment, if it's paid out after your death.

One of the benefits of investment bonds is that they allow tax deferral on withdrawals from the policy and can be used in effective tax planning, particularly for higher-rate taxpayers. You can draw up to 5 per cent of the original investment each policy year without attracting an immediate tax liability. The potential tax liability is deferred until encashment, when ideally you are in a lower tax bracket, or until death.

Offshore bonds

Many financial advisers don't like offshore bonds (available from offshore life insurance companies), but some maintain that they can work well for wealthier investors who have used up their pension and ISA allowances. It's possible to hold a wide range of funds within the bond wrapper (which can be thought of as a 'container' in which bonds or funds are held) and to switch between them quite easily, although you tend to pay more in charges than for an onshore bond.

However, the extra costs are offset by the advantageous tax structure. Profits roll up gross until the bond is surrendered or matures, by which time you may have retired and moved into a lower tax bracket. Like their onshore investment bond cousins, you're allowed to withdraw up to 5 per cent of your capital each year for 20 years and defer tax on it, although you'll have to pay income tax on any sum you take out over and above that 5 per cent allowance.

Venture capital trusts

Venture capital trusts (VCTs) offer some of the best tax breaks available – if you can stomach the risks involved with the underlying investments. VCTs are effectively companies quoted on the stock exchange that invest mainly in high-risk unquoted companies or start-ups.

The government has been keen to promote them in a bid to make Britain more entrepreneurial. And to encourage investors to put their money into such risky businesses, you get 30 per cent up-front tax relief on the investment you make, as long as you keep the cash in place for five years. This means that every £10,000 you invest will only cost you £7,000 because of the tax break. There's also no income tax to pay on any dividends or CGT to pay on the increase in your stake in the trust. And you can stagger withdrawal of funds to avoid paying any CGT you might owe.

The minimum investment in most trusts is around the £5,000 mark. There's no limit to the amount you can invest, but you can only claim tax relief on the first £200,000. Because the trust is quoted on the stock exchange you can buy and sell at any time, but you lose the up-front tax relief if you sell within three years. Remember, too, that if you do sell, you may get a poor price for your shares. This is definitely an area where you need to take specialist independent financial advice before investing.

7
ISAs in depth

One of your best friends in the battle to save enough to make your golden years golden will be individual savings accounts, called ISAs for short. ISAs are not savings products in themselves, but tax-efficient 'wrappers' into which you can put a range of savings and investments.

ISAs are an excellent way of investing for retirement. They provide a really good way of building up an easily accessible fund, offering good tax relief and flexibility. Importantly, you can use ISAs to generate a tax-free income in retirement. However, ISAs are a straightforward tax-efficient financial planning tool that can be used to plan for your future whatever your age, because they can be used to fulfil short- and long-term savings goals. For short-term goals, you can use cash ISAs and for long-term goals, stocks and shares ISAs.

The tax advantages of ISAs can help turn your pennies into pounds. Savers putting the full amount in cash ISAs each year, rather than an ordinary bank account, could earn a massive £73,611 extra over a lifetime – and the extra savings figure would double for higher-rate taxpayers, according to research from Alliance & Leicester Savings. So if your hard-earned cash is languishing in an ordinary bank or building society account, start moving it into an ISA straight away.

The great thing about ISAs is they allow you to save money for the short- or long-term, but you aren't locked into a particular timescale. If you change your mind along the way, you can cash in your ISA and spend the money on something different.

If you're using an ISA to save for your retirement at 65, but when you're 50 you need a large sum of money to deal with a family emergency, you can dip into your ISA. This flexibility is why ISAs are so popular. The downside is that you have to be very disciplined about the money that you have in your ISA, and need to resist the temptation to dip into an ISA for non-essential spending money.

A short history of ISAs

The Labour government launched ISAs in 1999 to encourage people to save for their future. They replaced the popular personal equity plans (PEPs) that the Conservatives had made a great success: more than one in three adults in the UK owned a PEP. Many continue to own PEPs, but they have now morphed into ISAs.

If you started investing before 1999, you may have some of the old-style PEPs. All PEP accounts automatically became stocks and shares ISAs on 6 April 2008, and become subject to ISA rules. PEP holders can still use their full annual ISA allowances.

ISAs have been very popular since their introduction, their main attraction being that any money accrued within them is free of either income tax or capital gains tax. ISAs are held by more than 16 million individual investors, with policies worth more than £180 billion. When the government brought in ISAs, they initially said that the scheme would only run until 2009. Thankfully, they've now changed their stance, guaranteeing that the existing annual ISA allowances will continue indefinitely. The original £7,000 limit on annual savings has been extended by an extra £200 – very good news for investors.

ISA basics

Higher limits for annual investment in ISAs came into force on 6 April 2008. People can save up to £3,600 in a cash ISA and up to £7,200 in a stocks and shares ISA, within an overall annual savings limit of £7,200.

Each tax year ends on 5 April and this is the cut-off point for investing. While you can put money in and take money out of an ISA during the year, you can't put in more than £7,200. And once you've taken money out of an ISA, you can't replace it.

For example, if you put in £3,000 in May, and withdraw £1,000 for a family emergency in June, you'd be left with £2,000 in your ISA. However, if your great-aunt then leaves you a £5,000 inheritance in September, you can't put the whole sum into the ISA – only £4,200 (because you'd already put in £3,000 in May).

Anyone over 16 may invest in a cash ISA, but you have to be over 18 to invest in a stocks and shares ISA. You don't have to be employed or to be a taxpayer to take out an ISA. Eligible ISA investments include cash deposits – including National Savings and Investments products – and stocks and shares including unit trusts, Oeics (open-ended investment companies) and investment trusts (see Chapter 10).

People with cash ISAs from previous years can transfer the money into a stocks and shares ISA. Savers who choose to make the switch can still invest the maximum £7,200 a year in their ISA that tax year. This flexibility can be useful, but bear in mind that it's not possible to transfer funds in the other direction (i.e. from a stocks and shares ISA to a cash ISA).

The changes mean some savers have a lower investment ceiling for their stocks and shares than they did previously. The new, raised, cash limit of £3,600 means that someone who chooses to save the maximum cash each year will only be able to invest £3,600 in stocks and shares – less than the previous limit of £4,000 a year.

How to use ISAs in your financial plans

Put enough in cash ISAs to act as an emergency fund. If you've an investment goal that's less than five years from now, use cash ISAs to build up funds. For any financial goal more than five years away, you can build up funds in stocks and shares ISAs. This might be your retirement fund. Or it might be a fund to put your kids through university. Or a fund to buy a new car, or pay for a round-the-world trip. Or just for a rainy day.

Something to think about

If ISAs do survive – if the government changes they may not – you could over the next 25 years put away £180,000 (25 × £7,200). If this simply grows enough to beat inflation and hold its value, it could at retirement generate an annual income of £9,000, assuming interest rates at the time are 5 per cent. Even if you can only generate an income of 3 per cent, you'll have £5,400 a year to add to your basic state pension.

If your ISA grows above the rate of inflation, the pot will be much larger and your retirement will be much more comfortable. You would expect your ISA to grow much more than inflation if it's invested in the stock market. If your £7,200 annual ISA investment grows at 7 per cent a year above the rate of inflation, after 25 years you would have £487,270. If you generate a 3 per cent tax-free income from this you would have £14,618 a year to live on in retirement. So simply putting money into ISAs over 25 years could get you the retirement income you desire.

Cash ISAs

You buy a cash ISA, essentially a cash savings account with tax advantages, from most banks and building societies. Many cash ISAs can be opened with as little as £1, and the balance is available to be withdrawn at any time, so there's really no excuse for not having one. If you want to build up a cash fund for emergencies, it makes sense to do this using a cash ISA as you won't pay savings tax on the money held inside.

If you pay tax at the basic rate, you would usually pay 20 per cent tax on your savings interest, but interest earned within a cash ISA is tax-free. For example, if you invest £3,000 in a cash ISA and the account pays interest at 5 per cent, you'll earn £30 more in a year than you would if it was in an ordinary bank or building society earning the same 5 per cent interest rate. In the ordinary account, the 5 per cent interest rate would become 4 per cent after 20 per cent savings tax, so instead of earning £150 in interest, you would earn just £120. If interest rates are higher, 6 per cent, then your £3,000 would earn £36 more in a year in the cash ISA (£180 interest compared with £144 interest in the ordinary taxed account).

Stocks and shares ISAs

If your goal is to build up a pot of money to rely on in retirement, you are a 'growth' investor. ISAs are ideal for growth investors because any capital gains generated within the ISA wrapper are tax-free. Growth traditionally comes from stock market investments, also called equities. You can put up to £7,200 in equities each year, either directly (in a self-select ISA, see below) or via a collective fund. Most stocks and shares ISA investors choose collective vehicles, such as funds and investment trusts (these are covered in Chapter 10)

Self-Select ISAs

Sophisticated active investors who want flexibility in their ISA holdings may be interested in self-select ISAs. Usually provided and administered by stockbrokers, self-select ISAs are designed for mixing and matching funds, equities, gilts, bonds and cash. You make your own investment decisions.

Self-select ISAs run by stockbrokers are for active investors who want the ability to trade within their ISA wrapper. A self-select ISA can hold individual equities, investment trusts, gilts, bonds and cash as well as (or instead of) unit trusts and Oeics. Stockbrokers usually charge either a flat fee for the ISA wrapper or a percentage charge of the portfolio value. Remember that you'll have to pay the broker's dealing costs as well.

Self-select ISAs vary, not only in the charges levied, but also in the range of investments available. Alliance Trust Savings' Select ISA is an inexpensive choice for investors who want to make their own decisions, as it has no set-up charges or annual fees. Visit www.alliancetrust.co.uk or phone 01382 201 900 for details.

Transferring stocks and shares ISAs

Not every stocks and shares ISA selection you make will turn out perfectly. And you might find the ISA you choose this year isn't suitable for your needs in five years' time. The good news is that you're entitled to transfer between funds, accounts and providers as often as you wish. But bear in mind that switching funds carries costs that will eat into the value of your investment. Some ISA providers levy an exit charge on ISA transfers, so you might be hit with a double whammy of charges – one when you leave the fund and one when you pay an initial charge to invest elsewhere.

How to buy an ISA

If you don't feel confident enough to choose an ISA fund on your own, you need to find an independent financial adviser who will make a recommendation based on a thorough analysis of your financial circumstances.

Armed with a little investment knowledge, however, you should be able to make your own selection. If this is you, there are several ways to buy your chosen fund, and it's best to consider all the options before committing your money.

In the case of some stocks and shares ISAs, you pay fees for the management of the investment. How you buy the ISA can reduce those fees. As some ISAs charge 5 per cent up front, plus ongoing annual management charges of around 1 per cent, it's really worth looking into how to reduce these fees, as even small charges can eat into your investment significantly over the years.

Understanding ISA fund charges

Fund managers levy several charges on your ISA investment. When you buy your ISA fund, the manager takes an initial charge, which can be as high as 5.25 per cent of the money invested. On a £7,200 ISA that's £378 gone straight away, before a penny of your investment reaches the stock market.

There's also an annual management charge to cover the running expenses of the fund, including trustees' fees, administration and investment management. Annual management charges are sometimes as high as 1.5 per cent of the value of the fund each year. This means that if your ISAs are worth £20,000, then you could be paying £300 a year to the fund manager.

ISAs to buy direct

There are two types of ISA that you can consider buying directly from a fund management group.

1 **INDEX TRACKER FUNDS.** These charge little or nothing up front and you may be able to find a fund manager who is offering a discount on charges.
2 **INVESTMENT TRUSTS.** These aren't commonly available through discount brokers or fund supermarkets.

When not to go direct

If you know exactly which fund you want, you could approach the fund manager directly, as it would seem the logical way to get the best deal. You would be wrong! By doing this, you'll pay the fees in full. The exception is at the end of the tax year – in February, March and April – when fund managers sometimes offer reductions on their ISA charges. In the strange world of financial services, and particularly in the case of ISAs, it usually pays to include a middleman.

Discount brokers, also called 'execution-only' brokers, are a good option for investors who don't need advice on their ISA choice. Such brokers are able to offer discounts on fund fees because they buy unit trusts and Oeics in bulk and are therefore able to negotiate good deals with fund-management houses. The discount is usually offered on the initial charge – the up-front fee that you pay when buying a stocks and shares ISA fund. This initial charge can be as high as 5.25 per cent of the investment if you buy direct from the fund manager, but discount brokers often manage to negotiate this down to less than 1 per cent.

Fund supermarkets also offer heavy discounts on ISA funds. They are similar to grocery supermarkets in allowing consumers to buy a variety of goods from different producers at one central location. In the case of ISAs, they make life a lot easier for investors as the ISA tax wrapper is held and administered by the supermarket rather than by any individual fund manager. This means you can spread your ISA allowance between funds from several fund managers. It's also much easier to switch between funds, because there's no need to move the tax wrapper itself.

Another benefit is less paperwork, as you just get one regular statement from the fund supermarket, rather than individual statements from the fund managers in whose funds you're invested.

Supermarkets allow you to view your ISA portfolio online. You can choose ready-made fund packages if you're unsure about making your own choices. However, note that most fund supermarkets don't sell investment trusts, only unit trusts and Oeics.

How to choose a stocks and shares ISA

You can put almost anything in an ISA, from cash, bonds and shares to commercial property and gold. There are thousands of ISA funds to choose from, so you're bound to find something that suits your circumstances. But it also makes your selection a bit daunting as you'll have to do a lot of research before you choose. Don't just go for the funds that are being marketed everywhere in that particular year. Investors who have been seduced by fashionable funds, such as technology funds, have suffered heavy losses in the past.

Experienced investors, or those who are comfortable with extra risk, take a view on the investments that will do well in the short term based on the economic climate. Someone may, for example, think that Japan is going to do well this year and so put this year's ISA allocation into a Japanese equity fund. But this is a risky approach to investing, as the judgement may prove to be flawed. Many investors who try to time the markets in this way end up losing money.

A more reliable strategy is to make sure you understand the principles of asset allocation. You then construct an ISA portfolio that is spread between different asset classes, to spread risk and hopefully still meet your financial goals. For more on asset allocation, turn to Chapter 9.

Contacts

Discount brokers

Allenbridge Group: www.allenbridge.co.uk

Bestinvest: www.bestinvest.co.uk

Chelsea Financial Services: www.chelseafs.co.uk

Financial Discounts Direct: www.financial-discounts.co.uk

Hargreaves Lansdown: www.hargreaveslansdown.co.uk

Torquil Clark: www.tqonline.co.uk

Fund Choice: www.ISAchoice.co.uk

Fund supermarkets

Interactive Investor: www.iii.co.uk

Barclays Stockbrokers: www.stockbrokers.Barclays.co.uk

Cofunds: www.cofunds.co.uk (only available through an independent financial adviser)

Fidelity FundsNetwork: www.fidelity.co.uk

FundChoice: www.ISAchoice.co.uk

Funds Direct: www.fundsdirect.co.uk

Hargreaves Lansdown: www.hargreaveslansdown.co.uk

Torquil Clark: www.tqonline.co.uk

Stockbrokers that offer self-select ISAs

Hoodless Brennan: www.hoodlessbrennan.com

The Share Centre: www.share.com

ShareCrazy: www.sharecrazy.com

Saga Share Direct: www.saga.co.uk

Halifax Share Dealing: www.halifax.co.uk/sharedealing

TD Waterhouse: www.tdwaterhouse.co.uk

Barclays Stockbrokers: www.stockbrokers.barclays.co.uk

Abbey Sharedealing: www.abbeysharedealing.com

8 Pensions in depth

If you want to make some decent retirement savings, you're going to have to tackle the subject of pensions straight away – if you haven't already done so. They can seem boring and complicated, but pensions can be your lifeline when you're playing catch-up in the game of saving for retirement.

Pensions are long-term investments designed to help ensure that you've enough income in retirement. The government encourages you to save towards your pension by offering tax relief on your contributions. Every pound you save in a pension is automatically topped up to £1.25 as soon as you put it into the pension. Higher-rate taxpayers have their £1 contribution topped up to £1.66. Instant tax benefits as valuable as this don't exist anywhere else in the financial system. The uplift to pension savings given by the tax relief you receive on your contributions shouldn't be ignored by anyone trying to maximise their retirement income.

Most people are confused about pensions. Although they're not rocket science, they do baffle even the most highly intelligent professional people, as the pensions system is extremely complex. In fact it's so complex that I once heard it said that only four people in the country understand it inside out. So there's no shame in feeling a bit daunted by the subject.

If you're regretting not doing more in the past to save for your retirement (and most of us are in this boat!) you'll find comfort in the new flexible pensions rules that began in 2006. These make it much easier to top up your pension. You'll also have more flexibility when you reach retirement. But when you're in your 40s, you need to be concentrating on growing your pension pot as much as you can.

How much should you save?

For anyone starting from scratch, pensions guru Adrian Boulding from insurance company Legal & General has invented a useful yardstick. He suggests dividing your age by two to arrive at the percentage of earnings you need to save to achieve a pension of two-thirds your final salary. According to this formula, someone who starts to save at 40 needs to put aside 20 per cent of earnings.

However, you may have already started a retirement plan. In this case, the official government and Financial Services Authority pension calculator at www. pensioncalculator. org.uk will help you calculate how much you need to save, taking into account what you have already saved.

To find out how much state pension you can expect, visit the Department for Work and Pensions website (www.thepensionservice.gov.uk) or phone the State Pension Forecasting Team on 0845 300 0168.

Pension rules

In 2006, the government changed the rules about the amounts that can be contributed to a pension. Fortunately, this now makes pensions simpler to understand. If you wish, and can afford to, you can now save your whole annual salary in a pension and wipe out your income tax bill for that year. Of course, most people won't be able to save this much. However, if you receive an inheritance or windfall one year, this does make it easier to top up your pension using these lump sums as they become available.

You can contribute as much as you like into any number of pension schemes subject to very generous limits, after which you don't get the tax relief. Each year, you'll receive tax relief on your pension contributions up to 100 per cent of your earnings. The annual salary limit that applies is £235,000 for 2008/09, but most people don't earn anything like this.

Employees' payments to an occupational pension scheme are normally deducted from pay before calculating tax – the net pay arrangement. Most other individuals make payments after deducting 20 per cent tax – relief at source – and claim any higher-rate relief from HMRC, through their annual tax return. There is also a lifetime allowance of £1.65 million in 2008/09. Pensions savings above the lifetime allowance will be subject to a tax charge. However, a pension fund doesn't pay tax on any capital gains or investment income. And between the ages of 55 and 75 you can take 25 per cent of your pension fund as a tax-free lump sum.

At retirement, most people buy an annuity from an insurance company, but it is also possible to withdraw an income directly from your pension pot (subject to certain rules and limits). People in final salary schemes will receive a secured pension for life paid out of the scheme assets.

Pensions for non-earners

Non-earners, such as children or women caring for families, can invest up to £3,600 in a pension each year and qualify for tax relief. This can be very useful to you if your spouse isn't earning and you have surplus income or an unexpected windfall.

Choosing your pension

Did I say that pensions had become simpler to understand? Well, they're still pretty complex animals, and come in different breeds. A key problem for people who want to save for their retirement is deciding which type of pension they should use.

If you're employed, it's likely that you have a company pension scheme. This is a good place to start saving. Some company pension schemes are better than others, but if you have access to a scheme through your employer, it's likely to be a better deal than going it alone. Economies of scale – you're sharing the cost of running the scheme with other employees – will reduce the proportion of your investment that goes in fees. Plus, most employers make a contribution to their pension scheme. Even if this is small, say just 3 per cent of your salary, over 20 years it can significantly boost your retirement pot.

However, if you're self-employed you need to decide between the various types of private schemes aimed at individuals: stakeholder pensions, personal pensions or self-invested personal pensions.

Company pension schemes

If you're offered an opportunity to join your employer's scheme and it's making a contribution, take the money and say thank you very much. It's effectively a pay rise – and if you don't join you're depriving yourself of extra cash. Even if you need to make a contribution yourself to get the employer's money, you should do it.

Company pension schemes usually require you to make a regular contribution based on a percentage of your salary. You may also be able to boost your benefits by making additional voluntary contributions. Research by consultants Mercer found that the average employer contribution to a defined contribution scheme was 6.8 per cent, compared to an average of 3.6 per cent for the employee contribution. While this total isn't high enough to provide the much-desired retirement income of two-thirds final salary, without the employer contribution employees would be facing a much poorer retirement.

Final salary schemes

Final salary schemes are the Rolls Royces of the pensions world – the best type of company pension – as all the risk of providing retirement income lies with the employer. They pay a defined benefit, typically 1/60th or 1/80th of your final salary for every year you work for the company. So if you work for a company for 40 years, you'd get a pension of between a half and two-thirds of your final salary. This pension usually rises in line with inflation for the rest of your life. Fantastic.

Unfortunately, most final salary schemes have either closed altogether or stopped accepting new members. Those that survive have reduced the benefits. The majority of final salary schemes still open to new members are in the public sector, which means they're effectively underwritten by the government. In fact, MPs have one of the best final-salary schemes of all.

However, private-sector final salary schemes are not without worry. The spectre of employees who lost everything when their employer, and pension scheme, went bust still haunts members of final salary pension schemes. Final salary schemes rely on the solvency of the employer to make payments to employees once they retire. So when some companies went bust, their pension schemes did too. It's quite possible that more companies offering final salary schemes will also go under. However, this shouldn't put you off joining a final salary scheme if you're offered the opportunity, as there's now a compensation scheme in place to protect members of final salary schemes. The Pension Protection Fund safeguards 90 per cent of your final salary pension benefits if the employer goes bust. Under this scheme, anyone who's already reached retirement age, or who's retired early because of ill health, will receive 100 per cent of their retirement income.

If you haven't yet reached your scheme's normal retirement age, you'll receive 90 per cent of the pension you would have received, subject to a cap of £26,935.70 at age 65. The cap affects high earners, but for the majority of people the package offers valuable protection. You also have to bear in mind that, for most people, 90 per cent of a final salary scheme is worth a lot more than 100 per cent of a defined contribution scheme. For further information about the Pension Protection Fund visit www.pensionprotectionfund. org.uk or phone 0845 600 2541.

Defined contribution pensions

This is the most common type of company pension scheme as there is no investment risk to the employer – the employee takes on all the risk of the pension assets losing value or not growing quickly enough. The employer pays for the scheme to be set up and usually makes a contribution on behalf of the employee, with the expectation or sometimes a requirement that the employee also contributes a percentage of their salary. The money is invested along with contributions from other employees, and when you reach retirement, you can take your bit of the pot to generate an income.

Although the benefits aren't as generous as final salary schemes, there are no worries about whether you'll be able to get the money you invest. Whatever is in your pension pot is yours, regardless of what happens to the employer. Your main worry will be whether the investments in your pension pot will perform well enough to give you a decent retirement income. If the stock markets fall in the years running up to your retirement, you may have some sleepless nights.

There are several types of defined contribution pensions:

■ **OCCUPATIONAL MONEY PURCHASE SCHEME.** You build up a pot of money with which you can buy pension benefits. Your employer has to appoint trustees to oversee the way the scheme is run, including selecting the pension investments. Your employer may also give you access to a personal pension that is set up on a 'group' basis, which means there may be lower charges.

■ **GROUP PERSONAL PENSION.** These are similar to occupational money purchase schemes, but there are no trustees, which makes them more attractive to employers. Instead, the employer has a contract with an insurer to provide the scheme. There are also benefits for employees – there's usually a greater choice of investments, and it's easier to transfer them.

- **GROUP STAKEHOLDER PENSION.** Stakeholder pensions typically have fewer investment choices than personal pensions. To qualify as a stakeholder pension, the government's rules mean they must have an annual management charge of 1.5 per cent or less for the first 10 years, after which it can go no higher than 1 per cent. They must accept contributions of as little as £20.

- **GROUP SELF-INVESTED PERSONAL PENSION.** These offer a wider investment choice than the group personal pension. Through them you can invest in funds, shares, gilts and corporate bonds etc. Sometimes these schemes are offered to company directors, with a more basic stakeholder or group personal pension offered to other employees.

Rules applying specifically to company schemes

A rule change introduced in April 2006 allows you to run another pension alongside your occupational scheme. 'Full concurrency' means that you can pay into another scheme at the same time as your employer pays into your company scheme. Contributing to the company scheme is the only way to receive the employer's contribution, even if your employer's defined contribution scheme is lacklustre. So you could run a self-invested personal pension (a Sipp, see below) alongside your company scheme if you wish to take advantage of more exciting investment options.

If you're a member of a company pension scheme, you no longer have to leave your job to draw a pension. You may also be able to draw all or some of your pension while still working full- or part-time for the same employer, depending on your pension scheme's rules.

Flexible transfer rules can allow you to move money easily from a defined contribution scheme into another pension, if you want broader investment choices.

Circumstances in which you should *not* join a company pension scheme

■ **If you've already reached the maximum limit for the amount you can put in a pension** – currently £1.65 million (2008/09), so not a problem for most employees – you need to take action. If you go over the limit, the excess will be taxed at 55 per cent.

■ **If you've real difficulties affording contributions,** then you should opt out. But be really sure that you can't set up the minimum regular contribution – perhaps you could make some cutbacks elsewhere? – as it's worth doing it to get an employer contribution.

■ **If you're going to be caught by means-testing.** In some cases, paying small amounts into a private pension only serves to cancel out eligibility to state retirement benefits, such as the pension credit.

People on low incomes or those starting their pension planning in their 50s could find themselves falling into the means-testing trap in particular. You're going to need a pension pot of roughly around £100,000 to beat the pension credit minimum income guarantee of £124.50 a week. If you think you're going to save less than this, you probably need to take some independent financial advice on this subject. The adviser will look at the interplay between the state pension that you can expect and your private savings.

Personal pensions

With a personal pension, you pay a regular amount – usually every month – or a lump sum to a pension provider who then invests it on your behalf. The fund is usually run by financial organisations such as building societies, banks, insurance companies and fund managers.

The final value of your pension fund will depend on how much you've contributed and how well the fund's investments have performed. The companies that run these pensions charge you for starting up and running your pension. Fees are normally deducted automatically from your fund every year.

Personal pensions are suitable if:

- you're self-employed
- you aren't working but can afford to pay for a pension

- your employer doesn't offer a company pension scheme
- you don't want to pay into a company pension
- you're on a reasonable income and wish to top up your company pension

There are several types of personal pensions:

1   Stakeholder pensions

The basics

Stakeholder pensions are simple straightforward personal pensions that you put money into and can then forget about. You don't need to worry about making investment choices as your money can go into something called a 'default fund', where your money is first invested in the stock market and then gradually moved into lower-risk bonds as you come within 5–10 years of your chosen retirement date. They're the cheapest option for investors who want to make a modest level of regular contributions – up to £300 a month, say – and who don't want to be tied into saving for a particular term.

All stakeholder pension providers must stick to the same rules, so choosing between companies is relatively simple. The government rules for stakeholder pensions mean that charges on the underlying investments are limited to a maximum of 1.5 per cent a year for the first 10 years and

1 per cent thereafter. The minimum investment is just £20, and you aren't compelled to contribute regularly. Also, if you want to transfer your money elsewhere there are no penalties. Basically, the main attractions of stakeholder pensions are low charges and flexibility.

You can buy a stakeholder pension from most insurance companies. As the rules laid down by the government mean that all stakeholder pensions are pretty similar, you won't go far wrong by going to one of the household name insurers to buy your pension. Think of the major brands such as Standard Life, Scottish Widows, Legal & General, Friends Provident, Norwich Union etc.

Investment options

Stakeholder pensions must by law provide a 'default fund' for people who don't want to make their own investment choices. This fund must have a 'lifestyle' profile, which means that your premiums are mainly invested in shares – high-risk investments – to begin with but as you approach your chosen retirement date your money is moved into safer, fixed-interest investments. According to Legal & General, a leading provider of stakeholder pensions, around 8 in 10 savers choose the default fund. The main difference between stakeholder providers is in the number of extra investment funds provided within the pension. Some companies offer just two or three options, others provide a much wider choice, sometimes including funds managed by expert external fund managers. Most stakeholder providers offer UK and overseas equity funds, plus ethical, property, bond and cash funds.

Stakeholder through your employer

When stakeholder pensions were launched, it became compulsory for employers without existing pension schemes in place for their employees to offer a stakeholder scheme to staff. Some companies simply offer access to a stakeholder scheme and find that most employees ignore the brochures that they're given. However, firms that are prepared to make a contribution to the stakeholder pension scheme on their employees' behalf find that take-up is higher.

You can compare different stakeholder pension schemes by using the Financial Services Authority's comparative tables at www.fsa.go.uk/tables. The Pensions Regulator has a register of stakeholder schemes at www.thepensions regulator.gov.uk/stakeholderpensions.

2 Self-invested personal pensions (Sipps)

Once upon a time, insurance companies ruled personal pensions and almost had a monopoly on the market. However, in 1989 along came the self-invested personal pension (Sipp), and investors could claim back control of their retirement funding.

It happened a while back, but most people in their 40s will remember the Equitable Life scandal. The world's oldest life insurer came unstuck in 2000 after making promises to policyholders that it couldn't afford to keep. As a result, an increasing number of people have decided they don't want to trust their retirement saving to an insurance company. And many people now want to make their own investment decisions. If you think you can do better than the 'experts' at investing, then a Sipp is probably the right pension choice.

When Sipps were introduced in 1989, they were regarded as products for wealthy and sophisticated investors. However, do-it-yourself retirement planning has seen a recent surge in popularity among people with smaller amounts to invest and even those starting to save for retirement. As a general rule, though, Sipps aren't normally recommended for people with less than £50,000 in their pension fund.

An appealing attribute of Sipps is that they address one of the big problems of traditional pensions run by insurance companies – lack of choice. Sipps are a good way to keep control over your investments; you're in the driving seat for all investment decisions.

Self-invested personal pensions offer ultimate investment freedom. They allow you to invest your pension fund in a wide range of investments, including not only unit trusts, Oeics and investment trusts, but also individual shares, commercial property, gold and more.

As a halfway house, some pension providers, such Standard Life, offer personal pensions that are 'deferred Sipps' starting off in collective funds but that can be extended into other investments later when the total fund has grown larger.

A Sipp is really just a tax wrapper. The tax relief offered on Sipps is the same as for any other pension scheme. You gain tax relief at your highest rate on contributions – so if you're a basic rate taxpayer and pay in £80 to your Sipp, the government will top it up to £100 with an extra £20. If you're a higher rate taxpayer you pay only £60 of every £100: the government adds £20 initially and then you can claim a further £20 on your tax return. Like other pensions, when you reach retirement you can take up to 25 per cent of the fund value as tax-free cash.

Even if you're not earning, and therefore not paying income tax, you can still put up to £3,600 a year into a Sipp and receive basic-rate tax relief on it – which means you only have to contribute £2,880 and the taxman will fork out the rest.

In the mid-1990s, Sipp providers usually set minimum portfolio limits of £50,000, or £500 a month for regular savers. However, nowadays you can start a Sipp with as little as £50 a month. A new breed of low-cost, execution-only (in other words, you don't get advice) online Sipp providers has emerged. These providers offer low set-up and administration costs, plus access to cheap online share dealing and discounted investment funds.

Administration charges are influenced by the assets you choose for your pension pot. Many online Sipps have no set-up fees and low annual charges. However, they restrict your choice of investments mainly to investment funds and individual company shares. If you want to put commercial property in your Sipp, you'll probably have to pay a good deal more in management charges.

Investments that may go in a Sipp

The types of investment that you'll actually be able to invest in will depend on the type of Sipp you have. They can roughly be split into three groups:

1 **Low-cost Sipps.** These give access to collective investments and direct equities through an investment manager.

2   **Sipps from insurance companies.** These companies will usually require some investment in their own pension funds but will allow investments in direct equities, and some allow property investments.

3   **Sipps from specialist providers.** They will allow most types of investment including direct equities and property.

The full list of HMRC-permitted investments includes:

- stocks and shares (equities, gilts, debentures) quoted on the London Stock Exchange, including those traded on the Alternative Investment Market (AIM)
- stocks and shares traded on a recognised overseas stock exchange
- unit trusts, open-ended investment company shares and investment trusts
- insurance company-managed and unit-linked funds
- deposit funds (in any currency held in deposit accounts with any deposit taker)
- commercial property, freehold or leasehold, but not purchased from any person who is a member of the scheme, or 'connected to' that person
- traded endowment policies transacted with a person regulated by the Financial Services Authority
- futures and options, relating to stocks and shares on a recognised futures exchange
- warrants (equity)

- permanent interest-bearing shares
- convertible securities
- most tax-exempt unauthorised unit trusts within the UK
- land, including development land, farmland and forestry (but not residential land) within the UK

Personal accounts

The UK government has announced plans for a landmark new savings scheme to give all employees earning more than £5,000 a year the right to a workplace pension with a contribution from their employer. This new scheme is called 'personal accounts' and will open in 2012.

Most employees will be automatically enrolled into a work-based pension scheme from 2012, with an option to opt out. Employers will have the choice of automatically enrolling their employees into an existing pension scheme or into the new personal accounts.

Employees will see their savings in personal accounts matched £1 for £1 by a combination of contributions from their employer and the government. The employee will put in a minimum of 4 per cent of their salary, the employer a minimum of 3 per cent, and there will be 1 per cent from the Government in tax relief. For the first time, employees will have a guaranteed right to a contribution from their employer to boost the value of their pension pot.

Personal accounts will have low charges, enabling people to keep more of their savings. They will be run as an occupational pension scheme managed by a board of trustees, which will place the interests of members at its heart. Trustees will be advised by a members' panel and an employers' panel, which together will make sure that the voices of individuals saving in the scheme and of contributing employers are equally heard.

An estimated six to 10 million people will save in personal accounts from 2012. Unfortunately, some employers have said that they will close their existing schemes or reduce their pension contributions as a result of the reforms.

The Financial Services Authority has confirmed that the introduction of personal accounts in 2012 should not stop advisers recommending that an individual saves in the run-up to the new scheme. This means you shouldn't put off saving for retirement to 2012 – it won't be in your best interests. For example, let's look at a man aged 40 who saves £100 per month and retires at 65. Delaying saving for four years means he would have £20,000 less at retirement. Rather than have a pot of nearly £70,000, he would only have around £50,000. (This illustration assumes a 6 per cent investment return after charges.)

PENSIONS IN DEPTH

At retirement: annuities v. other options

You can have the best pension fund in the world, but if you don't make the right decisions about how to convert it to retirement income, your hard work over the years could all be in vain.

Annuities

Most people with private pensions end up buying an annuity of some sort with their pension fund. An annuity provides a guaranteed income for the rest of your life, which is essential for most retirees. You can make a vast difference to your retirement income through your choice of annuity.

If you have a personal, stakeholder or self-invested personal pension, or most kinds of company schemes (final salary excluded), you need to know about annuities. This can perhaps wait until you're near retirement age, but finding out your options early on might influence your investment decisions, and it might even make you question whether a pension is right for you at all.

The income you get from an annuity depends on various factors. It will be based on your age, sex, health and life expectancy. The older you are, the less time the insurer that provides the annuity expects you to be drawing an income, so the greater the income you receive. Men receive a higher income than women as they are expected to live shorter lives. If you smoke or are overweight, your life expectancy is reduced and your annuity income therefore higher. And if you've suffered a serious illness you could receive a much higher income. The technical bit is that providers of conventional annuities invest in long-term gilts (see Chapter 9), therefore long-term gilt rates will have a major influence on your income.

By understanding annuities and shopping around, you can boost your income by a significant amount. When you're about to retire, your pension provider will probably contact you, offering you an annuity. You don't have to accept this, and in the majority of cases, you shouldn't. You can buy your annuity from any company in the market, and annuity rates vary widely between companies, so you could be much better off buying elsewhere. The Financial Services Authority website at www.fsa.gov.uk/tables lets you check current annuity rates, tailored to your age and pension size.

Other retirement income options

Many people don't want to convert their pension fund to an annuity immediately on retirement. They may feel that annuity rates are poor at the time they retire, for example. Also, many people don't like annuities because the income from an annuity stops when you die, or a few years later if you paid extra for a guaranteed payment period.

There is another option: between the ages of 55 and 75, the government allows you to withdraw an income directly from your pension fund, within certain limits set by the Government Actuary's Department. You can also continue to draw an income directly after age 75, but subject to different rules. However, this is definitely an area in which you should take independent financial advice.

THE IMPORTANCE OF FINANCIAL ADVICE AT RETIREMENT

Converting your pension fund to retirement income is an extremely important – and often irreversible – financial decision, so you'd be wise to seek the services of an independent financial adviser specialising in this subject. Many advisers offer annuity services to help you secure the best deal. Some annuity firms only deal through financial advisers, so you may find that you'll get a broader choice if you go through an IFA.

Building an investment portfolio

Despite great effort spent in identifying the best investment opportunities, many investors ignore a key factor – arguably the most important – in achieving investment success. This is the need to construct a portfolio that is diversified across different investment styles, sectors and types of investments. In the jargon of the professionals, this is called 'asset allocation'.

Imagine your investment portfolio is a cake mixture and you'll have a better handle on how it's put together. Some ingredients are cash, some are company shares, some are made from government bonds, and a few may even be solid gold. You need a good mixture to get the recipe right.

Research has found that asset allocation – the practice of splitting your investment portfolio among different assets such as cash, equities, bonds, property and commodities – is the key to investment success. Some academics in the United States managed to work out that 90 per cent of investment returns can be attributed to the asset allocation mix of a portfolio. Only 10 per cent is the success or failure of the professionals who are managing your money.

As mentioned earlier, there's no perfect formula for investment success – otherwise everyone would be rich. But the diversification that lies at the heart of asset allocation is very straightforward. In simple terms, if you don't put all your eggs in one basket, you're less likely to lose your money.

The theory is that you can reduce the risk of your portfolio not growing in the desired way because each asset type performs in a different way from the others. Certain assets respond better or worse in different economic conditions. When equities rise, for example, bonds often fall. And when the stock market begins to fall, commercial property might start to generate stronger returns. This doesn't always work, of course, but it generally holds true.

The basic ingredients of an investment portfolio

Cash

Most 40-somethings have some money on deposit in a bank account. Great. This is the basis of your portfolio.

Cash is simple: you put your money in a bank or building society and get it back with interest on top. Most investors need a cash cushion to pay for emergencies, such as a new washing machine, or to tide them over if they become unexpectedly unemployed. Ideally, you should have between three and six months' income saved in an emergency cash fund that you can access easily. Obviously, it's very important to get a decent rate of interest, particularly one that beats the current rate of inflation, otherwise the cash element of your portfolio will be losing its value. You can find the best rates for your savings at www.moneyfacts.co.uk.

Equities

Equities – another word for shares – often seem frightening to the beginner investor, and the stock market can seem daunting and complicated. But you may already own equities without realising it: for example, if you're a member of a company pension scheme. Equities are simply a way of sharing in the growth of the economy, and by buying shares you are buying a stake in a company.

If the company is a successful business, the value of your shares could rise and you might be able to sell them at a profit. If the company does badly, your shares may fall in value. Equities are considered to be high-risk investments as there's always a chance you might not get your money back – if the company runs into trouble, the shares may cease to have any value at all.

Equities are often used for investment growth. If you invest in the shares of a small company and it grows into a multi-million-pound enterprise then your shares will probably rise in value. However, equities can also be used to generate a regular income. They pay a share of the company profits to shareholders through regular income payments, known as dividends. Dividends can provide an income, or you can reinvest them in more shares to grow your capital.

If you're investing for the long term, experts recommend that equities form the bulk of your investments because, although they may go up and down in value from month to month and from year to year, history has shown that they provide the best returns of all the assets over the long term. Because equities are 'volatile' (they can rise and fall in value very quickly) they don't suit short investment periods, unless you're comfortable with a very high-risk strategy.

The proportion of a portfolio that goes into equities is the key factor in determining its risk profile. Very few people are truly high-risk investors. If your whole investment is in equities, you risk losing everything. For most, therefore, an all-equity portfolio is unsuitable, although at 40 you have many years to retirement so would usually be advised to put the majority of your investment in equities.

You need to spread your equity investments between large and small companies. Small companies have greater potential to grow but are riskier, while big companies such as those that comprise the FTSE 100 index offer relative stability with some growth potential. If small companies do badly, your large company investments may be doing well and can thus maintain the value of your portfolio.

Most investors are far too UK-centric, perhaps concerned about committing to overseas markets. While the UK should always represent a core holding for any UK investor, it's best to spread the risk by also investing overseas. A global approach to investing can offer broader diversification and greater investment potential – and this diversification can lower the risk of your portfolio performing badly. An investment overseas might also offset poor performance in the UK. If you're investing overseas, you're also taking a risk with currency differences. For instance, if you're invested in, say, Japan and the yen falls against sterling, the value of your Japanese investments will be worth less in sterling. At this point it may not be a good idea to sell, but over the long term the yen should recover.

Bonds

Bonds are simply loans to companies or the government. They usually pay a fixed rate of interest every year and aim to pay back the capital at the end of a stated period. Corporate bonds are issued by companies to raise money to invest in their businesses. Gilts (gilt-edged stocks) are bonds issued by the government. Corporate bonds and gilts are traded on the stock market, which means their value can rise and fall. You aren't guaranteed to get all your money back under all circumstances.

Bonds provide a more regular income and lower volatility than equities (they don't go up and down in value so much). They can act as a cushion against the unpredictable ups and downs of the stock market, and often bonds don't move in the same direction as shares. This is why investors who are more cautious and concerned about the safety of their investments tend to allocate more of their portfolio to bonds than equities.

Property

Property is fascinating to investors because it's a tangible asset: if you own a property – or part of one – you can go and see your investment. It's not a piece of paper that can lose its value overnight, but bricks and mortar that will still be there tomorrow, even if they're worth less.

However, buying your own home doesn't make you an expert in the property market. Investing in commercial property is very different from investing in residential property. Commercial property – which includes shops, offices and industrial premises – is a core asset to complement shares and bonds.

The market can be subdivided into:

- retail – shopping centres and supermarkets
- industrial – warehouses and factories
- offices – office blocks and business parks
- leisure – hotels and leisure parks

And each type of property offers different opportunities.

You generally benefit from higher guaranteed income on commercial property compared to any income potential from residential rent. You generate this income through institutional leasing, which gives you a guaranteed, clear return for a fixed term. In addition, you have 'upward only' rent reviews every three to five years. And, of course, the underlying value of the property can rise and fall.

Commodities

Commodities are raw materials for production. They include agricultural products such as wheat and cattle, energy products such as oil and gasoline, and metals such as gold, silver and aluminium. There are also what are known as 'soft' commodities – those that cannot be stored for long periods of time, including sugar, cotton, cocoa and coffee.

As an asset class, commodities can diversify a portfolio. Most assets, including equities and bonds, don't benefit from rising inflation, but commodities usually do. However, as commodities are volatile investments – their price can rise and fall very quickly – they should only form a small part of an investment portfolio. For the same reason, they aren't suitable for all investors.

Asset allocation for your portfolio

When considering the correct asset allocation strategy for your own circumstances, you need to look at your assets as a whole – your home, pension, ISAs and bank accounts. Most people have the largest proportion of their wealth in residential property – something that's hard to avoid if you're a homeowner. Many people also have rather too much cash in the bank – something that's easy to fix. You need a clear idea of what level of risk is acceptable to you: can you afford to lose your money? Are you comfortable with the value of your investments going up and down over the investment period? Will you be able to sleep at night if your share portfolio falls in value?

Financial advisers offer widely differing asset allocation strategies to deal with different situations. An asset allocation model determines the amount of an investor's total portfolio placed in each class. These models are designed to reflect the investor's personal goals and risk tolerance – whether they need a lump sum in five years or

20 years, for example, or whether they are seeking income now or in 10 years' time.

With a little investment knowledge, it's possible to put together a basic asset allocation strategy yourself.

Model retirement portfolios

Years to retirement	Equities	Bonds	Cash
20–30	80%	15%	5%
10–20	60%	30%	10%
5 or less	40%	40%	20%
Source: Bestinvest, showing a typical IFA's model.			

The mistake that many investors make is to do the asset allocation work at the start of their investment career and then forget about it. But the key to successful asset allocation is to keep doing it over and over again. Make sure that your investment portfolio is suitable for your age and life stage. Research from fund manager Fidelity found that young UK investors are often too cautious and risk-averse in the early phase of accumulating assets. Despite young investors historically benefiting from a portfolio that is weighted to shares, the research found that fewer than half of those aged between 18 and 34 have any of their retirement savings in the stock market. Conversely, the research shows that older investors tend to take on excessive risk very close to their planned retirement dates.

Fidelity suggest investors in their 40s and 50s should consider gradually increasing their exposure to bonds as a way to moderate risk. The few years before retirement are a particularly good time to review the asset allocation of your portfolio.

Choosing investment funds

Most people who are investing for the long term use collective investment funds. The advantage of these is that your investment is pooled with other investors' money and is used to buy exposure to a wider range of stocks and shares than you'd be able to achieve on your own.

Buying units or shares in a collective investment fund instantly gives you a diversified portfolio. As you aren't dependent on the success of one or two investments, this spreads your risk. A fund manager, who is responsible for picking the stocks and shares that he or she thinks will do well, professionally manages your money.

Before you invest, take some time considering the difference between the types of collective investment vehicle – open-ended funds and closed-ended funds.

Open-ended funds

Most investors choose open-ended funds, which are more heavily advertised and marketed than closed-ended vehicles. These are the ones you'll see advertised on the billboards at mainline railway and underground stations.

Open-ended funds get bigger as more people invest, and

similarly they get smaller as investors withdraw their money. If an open-ended fund suffers a large number of withdrawals (called 'redemptions') then it will have to sell some of its investments to provide the money for the investors who are pulling out. Similarly, when lots of people are making investments, the fund has to buy more investments.

There are two types of open-ended funds: unit trusts and open-ended investment companies (Oeics).

Unit trusts

A unit trust is an investment fund shared by a large number of investors. The fund is split into segments called 'units', which investors buy so they have a stake in the fund. The price of each unit is based on the value of the assets owned by the fund.

Like most investments, there are charges that investors have to pay to cover the expenses of managing funds. These charges can vary considerably.

There are usually two different prices:

1   **the offer price** – the price you pay to buy units
2   **the bid price** – the price you get for selling units

The offer price is higher than the bid price in most cases. The difference is pocketed by the fund manager and is one of the ways unit trust managers earn money.

Open-ended Investment Companies (Oeics)

An Oeic is a company whose business is managing an investment fund or funds. It's similar to a unit trust, with certain key differences.

Oeics package their investments into shares rather than units. They issue shares, and use the money raised from shareholders to invest in other companies. When demand for the shares rises, the manager just issues more shares. Therefore, the number of shares issued can rise and fall as shares are bought and sold (similar to units in a unit trust).

Oeic shares have a single price – there is no bid and offer price like unit trusts – and they're similar to the collective investment funds available in most EU countries. Many UK fund managers have been converting their unit trusts to Oeics in recent years. One reason for this development of Oeics is to make it easier for fund-management firms to market their collective funds across Europe.

Closed-ended funds
Investment trusts

Investment trusts are similar to unit trusts and Oeics in that they invest in the shares, bonds or other assets of companies and provide the opportunity for investors to spread risk. However, when you invest in an investment trust, you're buying shares in a company that invests in other securities, rather than buying units in a fund.

Investment trust shares are quoted on the stock market, so you take a stake in an investment trust by buying its shares. Investment trusts are closed-ended funds – in other words, there's a set number of shares, which remains constant regardless of the number of investors.

Investors must appreciate the higher risks and greater complexity of investing in investment trusts. They carry a higher risk than unit trusts and Oeics because they're allowed to borrow money to invest: a process known as 'gearing'. An investment trust that's geared is a riskier investment than one that's not geared, because just as the borrowings can magnify the gains, they can cause any losses to be much greater.

The value of the assets held by an investment trust might be different from the actual share price. This means a trust's shares can trade at a discount or a premium to the value of the underlying assets. This exaggerates the pattern of share-price performance both upwards and downwards compared with returns from open-ended vehicles.

In the very long term, investment trust managers have the advantage of a closed-ended fund, which means they don't have to sell shares in a trust that they would rather keep when investors want to cash in their investments.

Active management v. tracker funds

The investment strategy and style of the investment is more important than its structure. For this reason, you need to get to grips with the two fundamental investment strategies: active and passive. You'll be faced with a choice between actively managed funds and index trackers.

This is essentially man against the machine. Human beings control actively managed funds; computers control index trackers. Which investment style has the qualities to win the race to riches has long been the subject of debate.

An index-tracker fund avoids the whole concept of research and analysis and simply mimics a widely followed stock-market index. The goal is to hold every share in an index of leading shares, such as the FTSE All-Share or FTSE 100. There's no attempt to outperform the index, to buy more shares in any company that's considered particularly desirable, or to reduce holdings in any share that performs badly. They employ no researchers or portfolio managers, as computers do much of their trading.

An active fund, on the other hand, employs researchers, risk analysts and traders. Active fund managers have the freedom to choose the companies they wish to invest in, based on their individual merit.

At an active fund manager group, investment managers and analysts around the world will look for companies in which to invest. They talk to company executives, analyse the numbers, and study the competition and the market. When they've decided to invest, they keep a close eye on the company performance, meeting senior management several times a year, and constantly review whether to hold on to the shares.

By taking strategic views of economies, active funds might increase holdings in certain sectors to take advantage of anticipated favourable business conditions in those sectors, or of interest rate movements affecting a specific asset class.

Not all actively managed funds try to time the market, but many do. The turnover of many active funds is often quite high, meaning that on average their entire portfolios are sometimes traded more often than tracker funds.

In theory, active funds are best placed to outperform in a bear market – when share prices are falling. This is mainly because an active fund can manoeuvre and adjust its footing as the investment terrain shifts beneath it. For example, an active fund manager can bale out of under-performing shares and replace them with better-placed stocks, or can move into cash and bonds, depending on the aims of the fund.

The charges levied by the active fund management industry have often come in for criticism. Tracker fans cite the exorbitant charges levied by active fund groups as a major reason to avoid them. If you're parting with 5 per cent of your investment up front as an initial charge to an active fund manager, this can have a huge impact on your investment's performance. However, there are ways to buy funds cheaply, through discount brokers or fund supermarkets.

There's no right or wrong answer in the active versus tracker funds debate. Investors' preferences will depend on their objectives and risk appetite. Putting a foot in both camps is sensible. This is often called the core and satellite approach: a tracker fund core plus active funds to provide more specialist or higher-risk strategies as satellite portfolios.

It's important that investors in index tracker funds understand both the index the fund is tracking and the strategy being followed by the fund manager. Most UK tracker funds have a bias towards larger companies. At present, UK indices such as the FTSE 100 are quite concentrated – dominated by financial, oil and gas stocks. If you're investing in a UK tracker, you're taking a bet on a few sectors of the stock market. The flip side of the coin is that many actively managed funds underperform the index that they measure themselves against. So you need to choose your active funds carefully.

If you're picking active funds at random, the chances are they will underperform. You need to do your research and get a good manager. Some active managers have restrictive mandates – for example, they might be restricted by the company they work for to only taking small bets away from the index against which the performance of the fund is benchmarked. It's usually better for fund managers to have greater scope to turn to the part of the index that offers better potential.

Investors must ultimately decide whether they wish to try to do better than the market (and open themselves up to the possibility of doing worse) or perform around the market level.

How trackers work

Tracker funds are a basket of equities chosen to reflect the make-up of a particular index. Thus a FTSE 100 index tracker will hold all 100 companies in the index, but this doesn't mean it holds 1 per cent of each stock. The funds are weighted exactly as the companies are in the index, so a typical FTSE tracker will be heavily biased towards the

largest companies that currently dominate the index. On a
daily basis, a computer trades all the shares in the FTSE in
direct correlation to how their weightings move in the index.

Funds that track larger indices, such as the FTSE
All-Share, find it's impossible to hold all the shares. There
simply aren't enough shares on the market at certain times.
In these cases, a fund might hold the shares of the largest
150 companies in the index, say, and pick the rest on a
sector-weighting basis. As a tracker fund aims to mirror an
index perfectly, its performance is measured by how
accurately it mirrors the index, rather than by how much it
can over- or underperform it, which is how active funds are
compared.

Tracker funds often come under attack from financial
experts when stock markets are in the doldrums. However,
when markets recover, as history dictates they will, investors
in tracker funds reap the full benefit.

Trackers also tend to be much cheaper than actively
managed funds.

Exchange traded funds

Until recently, if you wanted an investment that simply
tracked the stock markets, you had to use an index-tracker
fund. But in recent years, a new and more efficient way of
tracking the markets has emerged.

Exchange Traded Funds (ETFs) are simple, flexible and cheap, and are becoming more and more popular among private investors. They give you the chance to buy whole indices as easily as buying a share on the London Stock Exchange.

ETFs are not much different from tracker unit trusts, which are already owned by millions of UK investors. Like an index-tracker fund, an ETF mirrors the movements of an entire stock market, sector or commodity by attempting to buy shares in the same proportions as on the index they're trying to mimic.

Structurally, ETFs are a mixture of unit trusts and investment trusts. They're effectively fund-based investments that are quoted on the stock market. And because they're listed on the stock market, you have to buy them in exactly the same way as you would buy a share. This means you pay a stockbroker's dealing charges, which start from around £7 when you buy and sell. Unlike with shares, though, there's no 0.5 per cent stamp duty to pay when you buy an ETF. However, because they're open-ended, investors don't have the problem of shares trading at discounts or premiums to the value of the underlying assets.

ETFs are eligible for inclusion in ISAs, and have the lowest annual charges of all collective investment schemes. Usually, these charges are less than 0.75 per cent and can be as low as

0.3 per cent. Apart from lower charges, a key advantage of ETFs over index trackers is that they have 'real-time pricing'. This means that when you buy or sell, the price will reflect the value of the underlying investments at that time.

Conversely, index-tracking unit trusts are priced on a forward basis, so you won't know the price until the next fund-valuation point. Normally this won't be a major concern, but it can cause problems as you can't be sure what price you'll get when you sell. If disaster strikes, the price could drop dramatically before your sale price is set.

There are plenty of ETFs to choose from. These days you can buy into a bevy of indices based on property, overseas markets, dividends and commodities. With ETFs, you can invest in major global and European sector indices, such as the FTSE 100, and the S&P 500, which follows the biggest companies in the US.

Where to buy ETFs

Barclays Global Investors' iShares ETF brand caters for UK investors with its iFTSE 100 tracking the FTSE 100, but it also offers 170 other options including emerging market equity trackers, property trackers and some linked to government and corporate bonds. Exchange traded commodities are also now available

from ETF Securities. For further information visit
www.ishares.eu or www.etfsecurities.com.

How to research active funds

Actively managed funds have been around since the birth of
Foreign & Colonial Investment Trust in 1868. Today, there
are more than 1,600 actively managed unit trusts and Oeics
alone, and then there's a wide range of investment trusts.
The vast choice makes choosing an investment difficult.

The ultimate aim of all investment funds is to create
wealth for the owner. Unfortunately, not all active funds
cover themselves in glory. Many fail to outperform their
benchmark, and there are plenty of poor fund managers out
there. However, there are also some fantastic fund managers
who are more than capable of providing a superior return.
The question is how to find one.

Some fund managers are excellent, others not so good.
So you need to research not only what the fund invests in,
but also the manager's track record. Managers tend to move
around a good deal, tempted by lucrative pay packages from
rival management groups. Look for managers who have
been in place for a while, say three years. Hopefully they'll
stay with the fund for the long term.

If the manager of your money jumps ship to a rival, this
may be a trigger to sell the fund. But if the replacement

manager has a good track record, why not give him or her a chance?

Multi-manager funds

If you prefer to leave fund selection and monitoring to a professional, consider using a multi-manager fund. The beauty of multi-manager funds, at least in theory, is that rather than having to search the entire market yourself, you can simply buy a multi-manager fund that will find the best funds for you.

Multi-manager funds come in one of two forms.

1 **FUNDS OF FUNDS,** which invest in unit trusts run by other fund managers. If it is a 'fettered' fund of funds, the manager will only be able to choose from in-house vehicles. If it is 'unfettered', the manager can choose from all funds.

2 **MANAGERS OF MANAGERS,** which give a selection of external managers a chunk of money to manage. There is a pre-set framework for the fund that dictates how much of the portfolio is given over to equities, fixed-interest and other asset classes. The fund manger then decides which firms and managers have the best skills to run each part of the portfolio and hands out mandates telling each manager how their particular share of the fund should be run.

There are also hybrid multi-manager funds, which employ a combination of both strategies.

Multi-manager is worth considering if you want a one-stop shop: if you want to sleep well at night or only have a small pot of money, they make sense. But if you have £20,000 or more, it's better to build a bespoke portfolio.

Multi-manager funds are rarely star performers – many concentrate on sensible asset allocation, diversification and consistent performance. However, some fund-of-funds managers are more aggressive when it comes to asset allocation, while others rely principally on fund selection to drive their performance.

You need to be comfortable with potentially higher charges than conventional funds. On top of the ongoing charges for the underlying funds, there's a second layer of costs levied for the multi-manager's funds.

A multi-manager fund can be a little more expensive in terms of fees, but this may not be important, depending on what you're looking to achieve. Many investors find the perceived cost is outweighed by the benefits of simplifying their portfolio.

Do it yourself

There's nothing to stop you creating your own diversified fund portfolio containing a reasonable spread of assets. If you're aiming to put an investment portfolio together for your retirement in 25 years' time, perhaps include some growth and equity income funds, plus a property or natural resources fund – it's just a question of picking the right ones.

Once you've decided on your asset allocations, lists of fund recommendations are available from many brokers. Or speak to an independent financial adviser if you're not sure what's most suitable for you.

Growth funds

The managers of 'growth funds' adopt many different investment styles, but a growth strategy generally means investing in companies and sectors that are growing faster than their peers. The benefits are usually in the form of capital gains rather than dividends. However, many growth-fund managers look for shares where earnings are growing faster than the market average.

You never get 'money for nothing' with investments, so higher-growth products are best suited to those who don't mind taking on extra risk and preferably can wait more than 10 years before they'll need the money. Smaller companies can be a good choice for growth investors as they're generally at an early stage of their development and reside in niche, underexploited areas of the stock market that are ripe for expansion. Equally, however, a great number of so-called 'penny shares' disappear without a trace.

There are plenty of UK growth funds, but the best growth often comes from a global strategy that includes, for example, Asia. Emerging markets such as Brazil, China, Russia and India are often seen as a good choice for growth investors because they're generally underdeveloped territories, poised on the brink of mass expansion. This makes them ripe for future stock-market growth.

If you want to spread your risk, buy a globally diversified emerging markets vehicle rather than a single country fund. Investing globally means that you don't have to try to guess which emerging region is best placed to mushroom.

Income funds

There's nothing to stop you using an income fund as part of a long-term growth investment strategy as they can also deliver great returns. If you reinvest the income you receive from the fund, you'll reap the benefits of compounding. Equity income funds in particular are often recommended for investors who are looking for long-term growth.

Funds for all seasons

Not all funds focus specifically on either income-producing or growth-oriented assets. Some big global funds take a very broad-based view, with holdings in a wide cross-section of companies from many different sectors and areas of the world.

Some funds simply aim for good diversification, in some cases across several asset classes. Other types of investment such as structured products aim to provide nervous investors with the security of positive returns (or at least no loss) regardless of whether the stock market is doing well or badly – albeit at the expense of the higher returns you might get elsewhere.

Structured products

Structured equity products – generally branded as 'guaranteed' or 'protected' – are designed for investors who want stock market exposure without risk to their capital, and are prepared to sacrifice an element of potential returns to that end.

They come in various guises, but are typically closed-ended funds with a fixed term of five to seven years. They promise the security of your capital plus a return linked to the performance of an index such as the FTSE 100 or the S&P 500 over that period – say 120 per cent of the growth in the FTSE 100.

Capital protection is achieved by putting most of your investment into the safe haven of cash-like investments where it will grow to the desired sum by the end of the term. The rest of your money (after costs) is used to buy equity-based derivatives. These are clever and complex products that can be structured so as to pay out the promised return according to any uplift in the index.

Where to research funds

There is a vast amount of information about investment funds on the Internet. Here are two websites that can help you choose funds.

Open-ended

www.investmentuk.org: the website of the Investment Management Association has lots of useful information for investors, including information on the different types of investment funds, daily fund prices, and search facilities to help you find a fund or a fund manager. You can also search according to Total Expense Ratio (TER), which gives a clear picture of the total annual fund costs.

Closed-ended

www.theaic.co.uk: the website of the Association of Investment Companies has a useful guide to investment companies, plus a search facility to help you find an investment trust.

Profits with principles

If you're concerned about the impact of your investment and savings on the environment and society – as many people now are – you'll be pleased to hear that financial companies are catering for your needs. And you don't necessarily have to put principles before profits: the two can go hand in hand.

The first ethical funds were launched 20 years ago and used strict screening processes to eliminate companies that were considered 'unethical', such as those trading in tobacco. Back then, it was expected that if you had an ethical investment you would sacrifice investment performance, as you were narrowing down your choice of investments. But there's plenty of research to prove that this is now not the case. Many ethical funds do very well and can be considered good investments.

Ethical investing encompasses investments that have a very specific stance – on animal testing, for example. Plus it incorporates investments in companies that may not be perfect but are aiming to improve their track record on the chosen ethical issues. It does, of course, depend on how strict you are in your ethics. One person's ethics can be seen as another's eccentricities. So you need to make sure an investment fits your own views.

Ethical investing

Ethical funds use a variety of different strategies to select their investments. These are sometimes classified in shades of green, so bear in mind that the 'green' label doesn't necessarily mean these funds are environmental in their stance.

Dark green funds

These funds use the strictest criteria to select investments. They generally avoid companies involved in animal testing, tobacco and arms manufacture. Investment in oil, pharmaceuticals and banking is also limited. This process is known as 'negative screening'.

Light green funds

These funds use a positive approach to picking stocks. They look for companies that have a good, or improving, social and environmental record. An oil company rejected by a dark-green fund could be considered for a light-green portfolio if it makes an effort to help the environment, for example by funding research into alternative energy technology.

Light-green funds are generally less risky than their dark-green cousins as their managers can choose from a larger range of companies.

Socially responsible v. ethical investment

Some make the distinction between ethical funds that avoid companies through negative screening, and socially responsible investment funds that consider all companies with the aim of encouraging change. For others, the two terms are interchangeable. Socially responsible fund managers may 'engage' companies in a discussion about their social and environmental policies, using their status as shareholders to push for changes.

Ethical pensions

As pension funds own a large proportion of the shares in the UK stock market, they have great influence over many UK companies and have the power to persuade companies to improve their social and environmental records.

More than three in four British adults think their pension fund should operate an ethical policy, according to a survey conducted by EIRIS (Ethical Investment Research Service, see below) and the market research firm NOP Solutions. By law, all employer-sponsored pension schemes have to state their policy on socially responsible investment.

This includes the extent (if at all) to which they take social, environmental or ethical considerations into account in the investment selection, and their policy (if any) directing the exercise of rights (including voting rights) attached to investments.

This doesn't mean that pension-fund trustees have to take account of social or environmental concerns within their investment strategies, but they're obliged to state whether or not they do so. To find out whether your pension has an ethical or socially responsible investment policy, you'll need to look at its Statement of Investment Principles (SIP). This may be sent to you automatically, but if not then you can ask to see it.

You can also lobby your pension-fund trustees to adopt an ethical investment policy. You might want to write to the chairman of the trustees and encourage other employees to do the same. And you can always attend the annual general meeting of the pension scheme and make your views known.

Where to find advice

Not all financial advisers will have experience or expertise in ethical investment. However, firms specialising in ethical investment have grown rapidly and range from large nationwide IFA groups to small independent outfits. The Ethical Investment Association publishes a list of members on its website: www.ethicalinvestment.org.uk. IFA Promotion's website at www.unbiased.co.uk allows you to search for ethical IFAs. You can also phone 0800 085 3250 for details.

Social and environmental issues to consider

By applying your principles to your investment strategy you may be able to change the world, but remember that there's no such thing as a perfect company. If you're looking for this, you may never find a home for your investment. You'll probably have to compromise or prioritise your principles in order of importance.

Also, be aware that everyone's opinion of what is ethical is different. Here are some of the issues that, as an ethical investor, you may be concerned about.

Avoiding investment in so-called 'sin stocks'

Many investors want to avoid investing in companies that have involvement in the following:

- the arms trade
- Third World debt
- alcohol and tobacco
- pornography and gambling
- animal testing, intensive farming and fur

Environmental issues

Companies can respond to investors' growing concerns about damage to the environment by producing environmental policies, putting in place environmental management systems and reporting on relevant environmental issues.

Specific environmental issues that concern investors include:

- climate change exacerbated by greenhouse gas emissions
- use of ozone-depleting chemicals
- use of pesticides and genetic engineering in agriculture
- use of tropical hardwood
- air and water pollution
- nuclear power
- mining and quarrying
- use of fossil fuels

Climate change is expected to be one of the major investment themes of the next 10 years.

FIND OUT MORE

The Ethical Investment Research Service is the leading global provider of independent research into the social, environmental and ethical performance of companies and provides a great deal of useful information about ethical investing on its website (www.eiris.org or phone 020 7840 5700). It also has a directory of ethical funds.

Ethical banking

Banks and building societies have an impact on their local community and the wider world through their internal operations and the companies they help to finance. So the money that you deposit in a bank or building society could be being used to support activities that you object to.

It's becoming increasingly common for banks to have guidelines for their staff on major ethical issues such as Third World debt, lending to the arms trade, human rights, and lending to oppressive regimes. Building societies don't usually offer overseas or business lending services. More banks and building societies are becoming concerned with environmental issues, charitable giving and support for the community, and social and financial exclusion. For example, research by the Joseph Rowntree Foundation has found that 1.5 million UK households lack even the most basic of financial products.

Banks and building societies that take a specifically ethical or environmental stance include:

- **TRIODOS BANK,** which finances companies, institutions and projects that add cultural value and benefit people and the environment, with the support of depositors and investors who want to encourage corporate social responsibility and a sustainable society. It guarantees your money will *only* finance businesses and charities that benefit people and the environment. Tel: 0500 008 720, www.triodos.co.uk.

- **ECOLOGY BUILDING SOCIETY,** which is dedicated to improving the environment by promoting sustainable housing and sustainable communities. It uses the money deposited by savers to provide mortgages to those whose plans will be of benefit to the environment. Tel: 0845 674 5566, www.ecology.co.uk.

- **CO-OPERATIVE BANK,** which believes in taking action against climate change. Since 1998 it hasn't invested in any business involved in the extraction or production of fossil fuels. This is just one aspect of its ethical policy, which is guided by its customers. Tel: 0845 600 6000, www.co-operativebank.co.uk.

- **CHARITY BANK,** whose sole business is to accept deposits in order to make affordable loans for charitable purposes. Individuals can open up a savings account and know that their money is working for the benefit of communities. Tel: 01732 774040, www.charitybank.org.

Ethical mortgages

There are a few mortgages with an ethical or green ethos.
These are available from:

- **CO-OPERATIVE BANK.** This funds several Climate Care projects
  across the world on behalf of its mortgage customers. These donations
  make a significant reduction in carbon dioxide and so help offset
  the emissions of its mortgage customers' homes by an average of
  one-fifth. Tel: 0845 600 6000, www.co-operativebank.co.uk.

- **NORWICH AND PETERBOROUGH BUILDING SOCIETY.** This offers
  a special 'green' mortgage for new homes only (i.e. homes which have
  a Standard Assessment Procedure (SAP) rating of 100 or higher) or an
  existing property that you want to make more energy-efficient. For
  every customer who takes out a green mortgage, the society will plant
  40 trees to help the planet breathe. Tel: 0845 300 2511,
  www.npbs.co.uk.

- **ECOLOGY BUILDING SOCIETY.** This provides mortgages only to
  those whose plans will be of benefit to the environment. For example, it
  provides mortgages for energy-efficient housing, ecological renovation,
  derelict and dilapidated properties and small-scale and ecological
  enterprises. Tel: 0845 674 5566, www.ecology.co.uk.

Retiring abroad

More than 3.3 million British pensioners – one in five – will be living overseas by 2050, according to research from the Institute for Public Policy Research (IPPR). In 1981 there were just 252,000 British pensioners living overseas, but by 1991 that number had more than doubled to 594,000. And by the start of 2006 there were more than one million, with one in 12 British pensioners living abroad. Almost a fifth of the British pensioners overseas can be found in Australia, while the US, Spain, Ireland, Canada and France make up the five other top retirement destinations for British retirees.

On a wet winter Monday in the UK, it's easy to understand why people would want to spend their retirement in sunnier climes. However, it's not fun in the sun for every British pensioner abroad. IPPR's research shows that some find it difficult to adjust to life overseas and struggle to access healthcare, or find themselves lonely without local language skills. So, not every Brit enjoys their retirement in Benidorm more than they would have if they'd stayed in Bournemouth.

The fact is that retirement abroad isn't simply an extended summer holiday, and a vast number of issues need to be considered before you make the bold step of emigrating. Choosing your destination country is the first decision. You may be installing yourself close to family and friends who've already made the move, or you may be simply putting down roots in a place you've enjoyed a holiday. However, you really need to live somewhere for a trial period (or at least visit it at different times of the year) to find out how you would cope with the changing climate or the quieter environment off-season when some shops and restaurants may be closed.

Learning the language will help you settle in: the inability to speak the local language is one of the biggest barriers to settling into an overseas community. Perhaps surprisingly, fewer than one in four retired Brits living on the Costa del Sol speaks Spanish, compared to retired UK citizens in Tuscany, where almost three out of four speak Italian. However, the IPPR found that Brits in countries like Spain and Saudi Arabia tend to flock together, in contrast to those in English-speaking countries like Australia and the US where they tend to be more dispersed across the country.

According to the IPPR, close on 400,000 people of all nationalities will leave the UK each year to live abroad. Yet in 2005, for example, around 91,000 returned to the UK. The reasons why a move abroad might not work out are varied, but the level and depth of planning well before the move are certainly a key factor.

A survey by UKForex found that the happiest expatriates live in Spain, New Zealand, Canada and Australia. The unhappiest live in France and the United States, with 19 per cent and 14 per cent respectively disappointed with their new life.

Top 10 countries with the most UK pensioners
• 245,311 pensioners live in Australia, representing 23.6 per cent
• 157,435 pensioners live in Canada, representing 15.2 per cent
• 132,083 pensioners live in the United States, representing 12.7 per cent
• 104,650 pensioners live in Ireland, representing 10.1 per cent
• 74,636 pensioners live in Spain, representing 7.2 per cent
• 46,560 pensioners live in New Zealand, representing 4.5 per cent
• 38,825 pensioners live in South Africa, representing 3.7 per cent
• 33,989 pensioners live in Italy, representing 3.3 per cent
• 33,854 pensioners live in France, representing 3.3 per cent
• 33,034 pensioners live in Germany, representing 3.2 per cent
Source: Institute of Public Policy Research

Financial planning is key to moving abroad. Retiring overseas is very complex, and it's essential that you seek specialist financial advice before you fly off to spend your golden years in the sun. There's a lot more to retiring abroad than simply buying a house.

It's also important to look at how your pension will be affected by a move, ensure existing assets fit into the tax regime of the country you're moving to, plan for inheritance tax according to the succession law of your destination country, and organise adequate health insurance provision.

Pensions

Make sure you pay particular attention to your pension before joining the silver flight. Whichever country you choose as your retirement destination, you'll receive a UK basic state pension provided that you've paid enough National Insurance contributions (NICs) over the years.

More than 1 million Brits receive a state pension abroad, and the government will pay your state pension money into foreign bank accounts. As this is likely to be the foundation of your retirement income, it can be disappointing to see this frozen at the level when you leave the UK, even though your living costs will undoubtedly increase over the years.

Most countries have index-linking agreements with the UK government, which means that your state pension will keep its value and increase in line with inflation. However, you might think twice about retiring to Australia, Canada, New Zealand and South Africa: there, your state pension will be frozen and could lose its value over your retirement.

Any pension benefits that you receive in the UK may be affected by your move abroad: for example, you may no longer continue to receive pension credits – the government's top-up for poorer pensioners. The Department for Work and Pensions' GL29 guide, *Going Abroad and Social Security Benefits*, has further information on this.

It's essential that you contact your Social Security Office, the DWP and the NIC office well in advance so that they know you're moving abroad and you continue to receive your pension. If you move abroad before state pension age, check how this will affect your state pension benefits.

Your private pension

Be aware that the value of your UK pensions will fluctuate with exchange rates because they're paid in sterling. It's not normally possible for income from private or company pension schemes to be paid into foreign accounts. This means that money has to be paid into a UK account and then transferred abroad. It's up to you to make arrangements for transferring this, and you should remember that there'll be both conversion charges and currency risk.

The alternative is to have your pension fund transferred into a qualifying recognised overseas pension scheme (QROP). QROPs must have similar rules to UK pension schemes, such as allowing around 25 per cent of the pension to be taken as tax-free cash, with the rest as taxable income. A register of QROPs is available at www.hmrc.gov.uk/pensionschemes/qrops-list.htm.

People taking early retirement and moving abroad before they are eligible to draw their pension will need to pay particular attention to the 25 per cent tax-free rule. Currently only those resident in the UK are able to take 25 per cent of their pension lump sum tax-free. If you're liable for tax in the country to which you move before you start drawing your pension, you may find that this 25 per cent is taxable as well.

For more information, contact the Pensions and Overseas Benefits Directorate, Tyneview Park, Whitley Road, Newcastle upon Tyne, NE98 1BA. Tel: 0191 218 7777.

Healthcare issues

One of the biggest problems for people retiring abroad is that there's no NHS to rely on, just at the point where many people start to suffer ill health. Britain has reciprocal healthcare arrangements with some countries – notably those in Europe – but even these don't cover the full cost. Healthcare in France, for example, can be relatively expensive for British pensioners following reforms by President Nicolas Sarkozy.

You may need to take out private health insurance for your retirement if you can't get access to free healthcare in your chosen country of residence. It's too much of a risk to retire abroad without health cover.

Some of the major household names – BUPA, AXA PPP Healthcare and Norwich Union – offer private medical insurance to British expatriates. However, it can be a very significant expense in retirement. Insurance premiums for a couple in retirement can run to thousands of pounds a year, so you need to budget for this in your retirement plan.

Many British-based private medical insurers offer generic plans but divide the world into zones (such as worldwide including the US, worldwide excluding the US, and Europe) for pricing purposes. The policies are annually renewable, so if you find the service isn't up to scratch, you can move to another provider at the end of the year. However, if you suffer an illness that needs treatment in the meantime, you'll find it difficult to get the same level of insurance because companies will cover you only for new conditions.

Your private medical insurance should cover minor outpatient care as well as treatment for more serious conditions in your destination country. It's best to go to a specialist insurance broker, usually in the UK, who'll be able to advise on the right type of cover. Whereas an insurer would be able to speak to you only about its international policies, the broker will be able to discuss other options, such as local insurance policies, that might be more suitable for you. A broker will also usually be able to help with any problems that arise when you make a claim, taking some of the pressure off you at a time when illness means you aren't equipped to deal with stressful situations. Contact the Association of Medical Insurance Intermediaries for details of a broker who specialises in this area (www.amii.org.uk).

It's a good idea to have a health and dental check-up before the move and find out whether you'll need inoculations for the country you're moving to. Another useful tip is to take a photocopy of your medical records, available from your GP, or ask them to be sent to your new doctor. Ask your GP, dentist and any other medical specialists to renew all your prescriptions so that you can continue your treatment abroad. Check the prescriptions list the drugs by their generic names, as brand names can vary from country to country.

Banking issues

Think about how you're going to run your bank account while you're abroad. Offshore banking is widely used by expatriates, and you don't have to be vastly wealthy to take advantage of these services – most accounts can be opened with a modest £5,000.

The majority of UK banks and building societies have offshore operations, usually based in the Isle of Man and Channel Islands. They offer similar services to banks and building societies in the UK but with additional benefits, including 24-hour telephone and Internet access, plus multi-currency accounts.

It's also worth considering opening a local account in your host country, but bear in mind that the quality of local banking systems varies enormously. A local account will help with running your day-to-day finances – paying bills and so on – and could help if you want to obtain credit from a local provider at any stage.

Tax

Tax issues are at the heart of everything you need to consider before, during and after you leave the UK. There are three major arms of taxation that need a particular focus: inheritance tax, capital gains tax and income tax.

There may be savings to be made by sorting out certain investments or property while you're still resident in the UK, before you move. For example, it's often better to dispose of some assets in the UK, because the capital gains tax regime is more favourable here than in many countries.

You need to look into your tax status and be aware how much tax you'll pay on income received over your UK personal allowance. Many countries have signed double-taxation agreements with the UK, which prevent most people from having to pay tax twice. The IR20 guide from HM Customs and Revenue is a good source of information on this and other related issues.

The most important distinction you need to think about is in which country you are tax 'resident' and where you are 'domiciled' – there's a big difference. For example, even if you live all or most of the year in Italy, you're not necessarily domiciled there.

Domicile is a legal term connecting you to a territory that has a distinct system of law, for example, England & Wales, Scotland, France. This law regulates the validity of wills, marriages and civil partnerships as well as your exposure to inheritance tax.

Broadly speaking, under English law you are domiciled in the country in which you have made your permanent home. Unfortunately, there is no precise or agreed definition of domicile, and other countries have their own definition.

Domicility plays a particularly important role in determining liability to inheritance taxes. It can be difficult to change domicility, for essentially it means you're stating you have the intention never to return to the UK. You won't be allowed to be buried in the UK when you die, and you'd have to cancel your membership of all UK-based organisations, and sell any UK property.

Inheritance laws differ from country to country and you may find that your new resident status affects your plans for leaving an inheritance. It's vital that you take expert advice about how you structure your will abroad and take legal advice to ensure that your wishes are met. In some countries, the law dictates that your property is divided equally between all your survivors, no matter what you would like to put in your will. Property may also sometimes be passed automatically to your children, rather than your spouse.

Financial advice

The issues mentioned above are a very basic introduction to life as an expatriate, and your affairs will probably need some detailed advice on investing and taxation relating to your new country of residence.

It's incredibly important that you take advice from someone who specialises in dealing with expatriates. You can find a specialist expatriate independent financial adviser by visiting www.unbiased.co.uk.

Children

As you turn 40, you may not have children, or you may be planning to have them; you may have tiny tots, or you may have adult offspring. Pretty much anything goes, and these days more people are leaving procreating to later in life, when they have established careers – or eventually got on the property ladder.

If you don't have children, planning for retirement is much easier as you don't have as many conflicting demands on your surplus income. Those with children may find that it's even more difficult to find any spare cash. And they may find themselves torn between wanting to provide luxuries for their children, such as foreign holidays and private education, and putting money aside for their own future.

Women in particular tend to prioritise the kids. It's the natural instinct to want to provide every advantage and comfort for your children. But this can be a costly mistake, if you sacrifice some of your own future financial security for your children's non-essentials. And your children won't necessarily thank you for it, nor will they be happy to see their parents struggling to make ends meet in retirement.

Investing for children

'Saving is a very fine thing, especially when it is done by your parents.' Winston Churchill

Children are expensive. Not only do they need food, drink, clothes and shelter as they grow up but it's common for their demands on your finances to continue into their adulthood. They might ask for a lump sum to travel the world at 18, or expect you to put them through university, help with a deposit on their first flat or contribute towards a wedding.

With the cost of raising a child from birth to the age of 21 now topping a whopping £180,000 (according to Liverpool Victoria survey on the cost of a child, 2006), it makes sense for families to start saving for their children's future as soon as they can.

Children are also arriving later in their parents' lives. While a few years back it would be usual for your children to leave home and become financially independent when you're in your 40s, or at least in your early 50s, these days many 40 year olds have small children or even babies. So at the point where you start thinking about planning for retirement, you may also have to think about financial support for your family.

The likelihood is that at some point you'll face conflicting demands for your spare cash. Do you put it towards your retirement or help your kids get a decent education? Even if you try to do both, you won't be able to save up for every event in your child's life. You'll have to prioritise, possibly with the help of an independent financial adviser who can help you see the big picture of your financial situation, and weigh up the importance of your financial goals. Most financial advisers agree that where you have to choose between educating your children privately and saving for retirement, you should make sure that you save for retirement.

There will be other difficult choices, too. For example, you may have to choose between paying your child's university tuition fees and helping with a deposit on their first home. A financial planner may point out that it can be better to let your child fund the university fees through low-cost student loans and for you to continue saving to build up a larger deposit. This is because the financial planner can project your child's financial situation years into the future and work out that your child will save more money in the long term by having a smaller mortgage, as the interest rate on a typical mortgage is much higher than that on a student loan.

You'll also need to make sure that you don't prioritise your child's financial future over your own. Mothers are notoriously soft when it comes to their children. But unless you are fabulously wealthy, you may have to face the harsh reality that it's a choice between funding your children's 'extras' and securing yourself a comfortable retirement. Your kids won't want to see you struggling in retirement because you've sacrificed your own financial requirements for them.

But there are always ways to try to do both. Consider the cost of Christmas.

According to investment company The Children's Mutual:

- family and friends spend an average of £180 per child at Christmas;
- children receive an average of 10 presents in addition to those given by their parents;
- 41 per cent of all of these presents, or 46 million toys, will be out of use by March.

Why not ask your family and friends to give your children something that will last much longer than three months – a savings top-up perhaps? Your children probably won't appreciate it now, but they may thank you in years to come.

Reasons to save and invest for your kids

There are many reasons to save for children: even smaller-ticket items such as school uniforms and music lessons can mount up to large sums over the years. There'll also be occasional school trips and holidays to fund. However, it's the big-ticket items such as school and university fees that stop many parents from sleeping soundly.

Independent-school fees are increasing far faster than inflation, with the average day-school fee per term nearing £3,000. University students now have to pay tuition fees, which means that many graduate with massive debts – the average student owes £13,500 on graduation.

But the requests for financial help often continue into young adulthood, with many children approaching parents for help on to the property ladder, or to pay for their dream wedding. They may even continue to live with you during their 20s or even into their 40s. This can be both a blessing and a curse. Marketers call children in this situation 'Kippers', which stands for 'Kids In Parents' Properties Eating Into Retirement Savings'.

Big expenses

	Cost today	Cost in 18 years*
Deposit on first home	£17,600	£27,500
Wedding	£15,900	£24,700
First car	£7,500	£11,700

* These figures assume inflation of 2.5 per cent a year
Source: The Children's Mutual

Where to start?

The sooner you start investing for your children, the better the chances of greater returns. The problem for most people is that when your kids are young, you don't have much spare cash to save. But even small regular amounts can become substantial sums over 18 years if you invest in the stock market.

Your strategy depends on two factors – your attitude to investment risk and when your child will need the money you've saved:

1 **WHAT'S YOUR ATTITUDE TO INVESTMENT RISK?** Can you afford to lose your child's pot of money, and are you prepared to see your investment go up and down in value during the investment period? Investing in stocks and shares means you may not get all your money back but there's great potential for your investment to grow. Saving cash in a bank account means your money is secure but returns will only just beat inflation.

2 **HOW MANY YEARS ARE THERE BEFORE YOU NEED THE MONEY FOR YOUR CHILD?** If you're putting away money for your newborn baby's university education in 18 years' time, you can afford to invest in the stock market. Your investment may go up and down in value over the term but things should even out in the end, and history tells us that the stock market gives the best potential for investment growth over the long term.

Experts recommend a timescale greater than five years for a stocks-and-shares investment. So, if you want to send your child to a private sixth form in five years' time, or to university in seven years, put your money in shares.

For any event that's closer than five years away – your daughter's wedding next year, for example – you'll have to put your money in cash, in other words in a high-interest bank or building-society account. This means there's no risk of your savings plummeting in value a month before the money is needed. The returns on your money won't be very exciting but, importantly, your child's fund is secure.

Tax implications of investing for children

For parents who invest on behalf of their children, there may be tax consequences. For children under 18, annual interest above £100 paid on a child's deposits or investments set up in the name of a parent is treated as the income of the parent – and the whole sum is taxable (not just the excess over £100 a year). This means that an investment may incur a tax charge even when the intended beneficiaries aren't taxpayers. So it pays to use the tax-efficient investments described in this chapter when you're investing on behalf of a child.

Investments designed to help you save for a child

Some investments designed to help save for a child are excellent. Others are awful. Here are those worth considering.

Child trust fund (CTF)

If the child in question was born after September 2002, she or he will have a government-sponsored investment account called a Child Trust Fund (CTF). At birth this is kick-started with an endowment of £250 from the government. At age seven, the child receives a top-up endowment of £250. Children from low-income families receive extra payments.

Parents, other family members and friends can contribute a maximum of £1,200 a year to the fund. The money grows tax-free until the child turns 18, when he or she can spend it as they wish. If the full amount is contributed, a child may have a substantial nest egg at age 18.

Children can't access the money until they turn 18, at which point they have full control over how the money is spent.

How much might a Child Trust Fund be worth at age 18?

£250 contribution at birth and age seven	£1,188
£250 contribution at birth and age seven, plus £1,200 a year	£40,500

Source: Bestinvest
Note: The above examples assume an annual return of 6 per cent a year net of charges.

With a CTF, parents can choose the type of account, and when the child is 16 they can have a say in how the money is invested. You can move the account to a different provider or change the type of account at any time.

There are three main types of CTF account:

1 **savings accounts,** which invest in cash;
2 **stakeholder accounts,** which invest in shares but have features to reduce the risk;
3 **share accounts,** which are higher-risk.

Stakeholder was designed for the CTF and recognises that shares are the best bet for long-term savings. If you don't make a decision to invest the government's voucher in a particular CTF, after a certain period of time the government will invest it in a stakeholder account.

Importantly, a stakeholder CTF has safeguards, including low charges and a switch to less-risky investments from the child's 13th birthday. Basically, stakeholder protects against stock markets crashing just before the child reaches 18.

If your family can afford to make additional contributions to a CTF, it's arguable whether a CTF is the best place for these funds. There can be better choice and better value outside the CTF regime for top-up investments. The range of investments available within CTFs is at present limited, so to get the fullest range, you need a self-select

CTF, offered by a handful of stockbrokers. This will allow you access to all unit trust and investment trusts, plus direct share dealing. You make the investment decisions – the drawback is that you have to pay an annual plan charge, which makes this option more expensive than a unit trust or investment trust.

For details of CTF providers, including stockbrokers who offer CTFs, visit the government's website at www. childtrustfund.gov.

One big potential problem with the CTF is that the account belongs to the child. Many parents don't like the idea of young Olivia or Jack having full control of the money at 18 – and possibly blowing the lot on partying or a designer wardrobe. So if you're topping up a CTF, you need to be fully aware that you'll eventually lose control of how that money will be spent. You could be giving a child a large sum of money at 18 and he or she might simply squander it.

Unless you're absolutely confident that your child will be guided by your wishes in spending the CTF, if you want to guarantee the money is spent on university tuition fees, you'll need to invest it outside a CTF. Another problem is that you can't access the fund until the child turns 18. If you need money for private school fees or a school trip, the CTF won't be suitable.

Other problems include how to save for older children who don't have a CTF, and what to do if you're putting aside more than the CTF limit of £1,200 a year. Here are some ideas.

Children's savings accounts

Many banks and building societies offer special savings accounts for children. These often pay higher rates of interest than savings accounts aimed at adults.

There's no minimum age for a children's account to be opened. However, most providers require a parent or guardian to open and run the account until the child is between seven and 11 years old. Most children's accounts have to be closed by age 18, while a few can be kept open until age 24.

Many children's savings accounts come with incentives such as gift vouchers, but it makes more sense to go for an account paying a high interest rate rather than one with a low rate plus free gifts.

Most children's savings accounts are easy-access, allowing money to be withdrawn without notice or penalty. Some accounts require notice to be given before a withdrawal, to allow a penalty-free withdrawal. These accounts normally offer a higher level of interest than easy-access accounts. Bond or term accounts offer the highest interest but to receive this, the money invested normally has to be left in the account for a specific period. This could vary from one year up to five years, or some providers require money to be left until the child has reached a certain age.

It's a good idea to choose a children's account that's simple and has no strings attached, such as limits on your withdrawals, or interest rates which are made to look artificially high by the addition of an annual bonus that you could lose in some circumstances. Also make sure that you fill out a special HMRC form R85 so that your children don't pay tax on any accounts you open on their behalf.

Individual savings accounts (ISAs)

If you're not already using your annual ISA, you could use an ISA to save for children. For many parents, topping up an ISA is a better option than a CTF as it gives greater flexibility and choice. There are the same income and capital gains tax benefits. But with an ISA there are no government rules dictating whom your investment should benefit and when they should have access to it.

A potential problem with using an ISA to save for a child is that there's no line drawn between your own pot of money and that of the child. So you may be tempted to dip into the money for your own needs. It's also highly likely that you may be already using your ISA allowance for your own long-term savings – to build up a retirement fund, for example.

Funds and trusts

Fund managers often market specialist investments to parents and grandparents who are saving for children. However, you should be wary of schemes marketed to children as they may be mediocre – always make sure any scheme is going to be a good investment.

Note that any unit or investment trust can be used to save for children via a designated account or a bare trust.

A **designated account** enables you to keep control over the money you invest on behalf of a child by holding the investment in your own name but 'designating' it in the child's name. You are effectively ring-fencing the money for the child, but you'll be liable for any tax paid on the investment. The fact that you still have control of the money makes designated accounts popular with parents.

With a **bare trust**, the investments are still in your name but you hold them in trust on behalf of the child. The money is therefore the child's property, and is treated as the child's for tax purposes. Once the child turns 18, they can take administrative control. Bare trusts tend to work better for grandparents, as they can help with inheritance tax planning (with a designated account, the money is still counted as part of your estate).

In general, to invest in a unit trust you need £50 a month. Some funds marketed to children can be useful for their lower investment limits – some will accept minimum investments of as little as £25 a month.

Investment trust children's savings schemes can be a useful way for parents to capture the long-term potential of the stock market. The Association of Investment Companies can provide you with details of investment trust children's savings schemes. Visit www.theaic.co.uk or phone 020 7282 5555.

Stakeholder pensions

If you're thinking very long term for your child's future, you could start a stakeholder pension scheme on his or her behalf. The stakeholder rules allow parents to save up to £3,600 a year in a pension on behalf of a child.

This is the most tax-efficient investment you can do on behalf of a child. Because of the 20 per cent up-front income-tax relief (which applies even if you aren't earning), you don't have to invest the full £3,600 – just £2,880 (the government tops up the rest).

The magic of compound interest over long time periods – your child may have 60 years to retirement – means even small amounts can grow into large sums. A modest £1,000 contribution at birth could net the child a very useful pension pot of just over £30,000 at 55. This assumes the £1,000 attracts tax relief at the basic rate of 20 per cent, so that it immediately grows to £1,250, and then grows by 6 per cent a year net of charges on the investment.

The downside is that parents may not like the idea of tying up their investment for so long. Under pension rules, the child won't be able to access the pension until they're 55. Family life means that there may be unforeseen emergencies along the way that may call for cash. If your money is in a pension, you won't be able to access it.

Grandparents may find the idea of setting up a pension for their grandchildren attractive, as they are at the life stage to particularly understand the benefits of saving early for retirement. But grandparents can't set up a stakeholder pension for a grandchild without the involvement of the child's parent, because the parent needs to sign the stakeholder application form.

Friendly society saving schemes

Friendly societies have a rich history extending back to Roman times when they were created for 'mutual purposes' such as the payment of burial expenses for members. Today's friendly societies are mutual organisations, owned by their members, which exist to provide members (or their relatives) with benefits such as life and endowment assurance and with relief or maintenance during sickness, unemployment and retirement.

In 1992, legislation was amended to allow friendly societies to establish subsidiaries for the provision of a range of retail financial services including the management of unit trusts, open-ended investment companies (Oeics) and investment trusts, health insurance and life assurance, and investment products in a tax-privileged environment.

They're allowed to offer long-term tax-free savings schemes or investment bonds, up to a maximum contribution limit of £25 a month or £270 a year. The money usually goes into investment funds called 'with profits'. These invest in a combination of shares, bonds and property. Unlike conventional life assurance investment bonds, friendly-society bonds are not subject to income tax and capital gains tax.

Many friendly societies market these schemes as children's savings schemes, usually called 'baby bonds'. Parents can invest £270 a year for each child under 18.

Unfortunately, these products often suffer from high charges and mediocre investment performance. They're usually inflexible too: you can't access the money easily, as policies are usually set up for 10 years and there are heavy early-surrender penalties.

Critics of baby bonds believe parents can get better returns from investments in unit trusts placed in a bare trust. However, baby-bond fans stress the tax-free nature of the benefits and the peace of mind that comes from investing in a 'managed fund' and not having to take investment decisions.

Some baby bonds can certainly be useful as part of a wider portfolio of savings, if you have the time to research them and choose a decent product. As a general rule, though, it's wise not to make them your first choice for your child's investment.

For further information, contact the Association of Friendly Societies at www.afs.org.uk or phone 0161 952 5051.

National Savings and Investments (NS&I)

The government-backed savings bank offers five-year children's bonus bonds, which pay a guaranteed rate, free of tax. Children's bonus bonds are available in issues, and each has its own rate of return – which you should check before you invest. You can invest a lump sum of as little as £25 up to £3,000 per issue.

NS&I adds interest each year, along with a bonus every five years until the child's 21st birthday, all tax-free. You can invest in as many issues as you like, up to £3,000 per issue for each child. Unfortunately, at the time of writing the rates weren't particularly good, so you should check how they compare with the rates available from other savings accounts with other banks and building societies.

The bank also offers premium bonds, which offer the chance to win tax-free prizes. There's a prize draw every month with two £1 million jackpots plus over a million other tax-free prizes. The more bonds you have, the better your chances of winning.

Anyone aged 16 or over can buy premium bonds, and they can also be bought on behalf of under-16s by parents and grandparents. The chances of winning a big prize with premium bonds are slim. The prize rate, albeit tax-free, is lower than the rate paid on many savings accounts. And the odds of winning the top £1 million prize are very slim – you have a greater chance of winning the Lottery jackpot.

In theory, someone with the maximum £30,000 holding in premium bonds should win an average of 13 prizes a year, which should give you an average return of just over 3 per cent (at the time of writing) on your money – not fantastic but a lot better than some bank accounts. Although you won't lose your money, you may lose out to inflation if you don't win prizes.

However, if you want a bit of fun and a flutter, there's no harm in taking out the minimum £100 bond for a child, in addition to other investments. For further information visit www.nsandi.com or phone 0500 500 000.

Other investments

Some other more esoteric options come under the investing-for-children banner.

Zero-dividend preference shares (zeros) are a share class of a split-capital investment trust and can work well if you're investing for school fees. However, this product is as complicated as its name sounds and isn't easy to understand. You'll definitely need the advice of an independent financial adviser to explain how it works and whether it's suitable for your circumstances.

In essence, zeros are growth shares, which pay no dividend, so you pay no income tax. When the zero matures, typically after seven years, there's only capital gains tax to pay above the CGT limit. You can stage zeros to mature when you need the money – to coincide with the start of each school year, for example – but there is no guarantee zeros will pay out at maturity.

Bank of Mum and Dad: lending money to your adult children

If you're a parent of a young adult, or could be before you reach retirement, then you may face pressure or demands from your children to help them on to the property ladder. The Bank of Mum and Dad is one that likes to say 'yes'. So here are some ways to ease the financial pain.

Imagine your child is making a demanding request – the average deposit on a first property now runs to tens of thousands of pounds. Many parents do give money to their children to help them on to the property ladder, but this can take a huge chunk out of your retirement savings pot.

You don't necessarily have to give your children the money. You could consider lending them the cash, either as an interest-free loan or with interest on top. This isn't necessarily the best option, though. Can you realistically expect to get it back when you need it most in retirement?

Three in 10 potential first-time homebuyers anticipate financial help from their parents, according to research commissioned by the Council of Mortgage Lenders, which represents the big banks and building societies. There's always been some degree of financial help from family, but it's become more common in recent years and among younger households. However, a significant number of parents now expect their children to pay the money back. A survey conducted by Scottish Widows found that while one in 10 graduates receiving money from their parents was expected to return the money 10 years ago, this figure has now risen to approximately one in five.

With increasing worries about retirement planning, it's completely understandable that not every parent wants to part completely with capital that they might need in future. In your 40s and 50s it's probably time to be selfish and concentrate on funding your retirement, rather than giving away money that you may one day desperately need.

If you want access to the money, you're treating it as a loan, and need to decide whether to charge interest or set a deadline for when the loan is to be repaid. Some parents enter into a formal arrangement with their children. Others simply trust the kids to pay it back. A formal arrangement, though offering peace of mind for the parent, obviously puts more pressure on the child.

If parents are providing the deposit, the mortgage provider will lend less if the child is making interest payments, so parents need to loan on an interest-free basis. You could have a formal legal agreement or a 'friendly' agreement, which is more usual.

Guarantor mortgages

An option for cash-strapped parents that gets around the obligation to give away or lend funds is to be a mortgage guarantor. This allows your children to use your salary to help them buy a property, without having to dip into savings or investments to raise the actual cash.

Guarantors are usually parents or close relatives who pledge to cover either the mortgage as a whole, or any shortfall over and above what the buyer can afford to borrow. A guarantor must usually have enough spare income to cover the entire cost of the mortgage, irrespective of the applicant's own income. However, some lenders allow parents to guarantee just the proportion of the loan that can't be covered by the borrower's earnings. The guarantee lasts until the borrower is earning enough to cover the whole loan, at which point the guarantor is released.

Although this is a great way for parents who can't come up with funds towards a deposit to help children get a foot on the ladder, the main downside is that if the child fails to keep up with the payments, the parent will have to step in – and that could put their own property at risk.

Where there's a guarantor available, mortgage companies will often agree to a 100 per cent mortgage, which means the purchaser doesn't have to find a deposit. However, some lenders will only lend 75 per cent of the value of the property on their guarantor mortgages, meaning you have to find a deposit of 25 per cent.

Most high-street lenders now offer guarantor mortgages. However, if you're considering being a guarantor, use the services of an independent financial adviser and seek independent legal advice, as this is a complex area.

Lending to children: key facts

- Four in 10 first-time buyers receive financial help from their parents.
- Parents prefer to loan capital than give it away.
- A loan can restrict the child's ability to borrow.
- Gifting capital can impact the parent's retirement plans.
- Guarantor mortgages are a good alternative to gifting capital.

Remember to educate your kids about money

It's not the lack of funds from the 'Bank of Mum and Dad' that frustrates today's teenagers but more the lack of decent advice on how to manage money. Parents still tend to dish out the age-old adages 'money doesn't grow on trees' and 'save for a rainy day' which won't help their offspring master the necessary financial skills for modern life.

Research from NatWest found four in 10 young people feel they don't know enough about money management. And while money might not buy you happiness, expertise in managing it may well do, with 10 per cent of 11–18 year olds worried about the future and their lack of financial understanding. Personal finance is now part of the national curriculum, but it's bound to help children if their parents back up what they learn at school with some extra help at home.

Inheritance tax planning

Many people hope that an inheritance – perhaps in the form of the family home, or a portfolio of stocks and shares – will go some way towards funding their retirement. But did you know that if you're lucky enough to receive such a windfall, you may have to pay 40 per cent inheritance tax in order to receive it?

If an inheritance hasn't yet been received, you can't assume that the money will definitely come in. For example, if your parents are still alive, their savings or property may well be used up in meeting nursing-home expenses. Long-term care of the elderly is means-tested in England and Wales. Although everyone receives a contribution towards nursing costs, personal care (help with washing, dressing and feeding) is means-tested. Unless you have capital of below £22,250, you will not be entitled to assistance from the State towards your personal care costs. Nursing home fees can be as much as £30,000 a year, which can eat into family finances substantially, leaving little for the next generation to inherit.

Inheritance tax (IHT) may not be something that concerns you or your parents. After all, it's paid on your estate after you die, so it won't affect you directly! Many people view it as a 'good' tax, that ensures vast wealth is not passed on down the generations, creating a social divide between those who inherit and those who do not. However, for many people inheritance tax is a great irritant, particularly if they've worked hard all their life to accumulate assets that they'd like to pass to their children and grandchildren. In fact, a survey by MSN Money revealed that inheritance tax is now the third most-hated tax after council tax and fuel duty.

Inheritance tax planning is something that many people don't think about until they retire. So when you're investing in your 40s, it's more likely to concern your parents than yourself. But you could be affected if you're counting on a large inheritance to boost your retirement fortunes. It's perhaps something to discuss with your parents or other relatives, though it can be a sensitive subject to broach.

Inheritance tax basics

When a person dies, they have a certain value of assets that they can leave to their heirs free of tax. In the 2008/09 tax year this IHT threshold is £312,000. Inheritance tax at 40 per cent must be paid on the surplus. Any IHT liability is paid by beneficiaries of the deceased person's will, often at a time when they're grieving over a lost friend or family member.

Four in 10 households are at risk of paying IHT, according to research by insurer Scottish Widows. This is principally because the inheritance tax-free threshold has not kept pace with rocketing house prices. If your estate – which includes the family home – is worth more than the IHT threshold, your heirs will have to pay 40 per cent tax on the surplus. In 2008/09, when the threshold is £312,000, an estate of £600,000 carries an IHT bill of £115,200.

The government has announced the IHT nil-rate bands for the following tax years:

- **2009/10** £325,000
- **2010/11** £350,000

It's also now possible to transfer unused nil-rate band allowances between spouses or civil partners. This effectively means they have double the allowance. When someone dies, they can leave their estate to a spouse or a civil partner free of inheritance tax. However, they also transfer their nil-rate inheritance tax allowance to the spouse or civil partner.

The amount of the nil-rate band potentially available for transfer will be based on the proportion of the nil-rate band unused when the first spouse or civil partner died. If on the first death the chargeable estate is £150,000 and the nil-rate band is £300,000, then 50 per cent of the original nil-rate band is unused. If the nil-rate band when the surviving spouse dies is £350,000, then that would be increased by 50 per cent to £525,000.

Reducing your IHT bill

There are, however, several ways to reduce the tax burden for your family. The first is to write a tax-efficient will. For this you will need the advice of a solicitor and an independent financial adviser.

If you don't manage to write a tax-efficient will before you die, all is not lost, as your family can rewrite it on your behalf, using a deed of variation. A deed of variation effectively allows the beneficiaries of a will to agree among themselves that the will should be rewritten, so that assets pass in a direction other than that set out in the will.

You can also reduce IHT by investing in assets that qualify for business-property relief, as these are exempt from IHT after a two-year holding period. Business-property relief applies to most shares listed on the Alternative Investment Market (AIM). These are shares in small risky companies. Given the difficulties involved in trying to run your own

AIM portfolio, it might be better to use a professionally managed AIM portfolio service. The manager should seek to ensure that companies qualify for business-property relief, as well as attempting to deliver a decent investment performance. AIM portfolio managers tend to focus on established, profitable companies, avoiding start-ups.

Holdings bought under the Enterprise Investment Scheme (EIS) are also exempt from IHT after two years. EIS companies must have gross assets worth no more than £7 million at the time of investment, so these are very small companies and could be very risky. However, you could use an EIS portfolio service to reduce the risk. For more on AIM and EIS portfolio services, visit www.tax-shelter-report.co.uk. You could also take out life insurance to compensate your beneficiaries for the inheritance tax they may have to pay.

Key inheritance tax exemptions

- **TRANSFERS BETWEEN SPOUSES**. No IHT is paid on any transfer of assets from husband to wife, or vice versa, or between civil partners.

- **ANNUAL GIFT OF £3,000**. You can give away up to £3,000 worth of gifts every year to whomever you like. If you can afford to do so, you should try to use this exemption every year.

- **GIFTS OUT OF INCOME**. Regular gifts out of surplus income, as opposed to capital, are exempt from IHT. This is a little-used but useful exemption. Gifts do need to be regular, and properly documented.

- **SMALL GIFTS OF UP TO £250**. This is £250 per person, but it cannot be the same person you gave the £3,000 annual gift to. This is useful if you have plenty of cash and several grandchildren.

- **GIFTS ON MARRIAGE**. You can give £5,000 to your own child on their marriage, £2,500 to your grandchild and £1,000 to anyone else. This only applies to one marriage per person.

- **GIFTS TO CHARITIES**. Any gifts to charities are exempt from IHT.

Potentially exempt transfers

Most gifts in excess of the exemptions above made during your lifetime are exempt at the time that they're made, but are subject to your surviving for seven years after the gift is made. If you do survive the full seven years, there's no liability to IHT. If you die within this period of time, IHT will be payable. It may be at a reduced rate, but this only takes effect if you have given assets away within three to seven years of your death.

Gifts and tax: time limits

Years between gift and death	% of full IHT rate chargeable
0–3	100
3–4	80
4–5	60
5–6	40
6–7	20
over 7 years	nil

Tax-saving actions

The most popular actions people have taken to mitigate inheritance tax:

Making a will	62%
Setting up a discretionary will trust	32%
Visiting a financial adviser	28%
Changing ownership of the home to tenants in common	28%
Giving an annual gift up to £3,000	23%
Making a lifetime gift to friends/relatives/charity/trust	21%

Source: 2006 research by YouGov on behalf of Scottish Widows

Useful contacts

General
Financial Services Authority

The FSA is the independent watchdog set up by the government to regulate financial services and protect consumer rights. It provides information about financial matters on its website, where you will find information and comparison tools on pension and retirement options as well as a directory of regulated advisers and companies.

The FSA Consumer Helpline can answer general queries about financial products.

0845 606 1234/www.fsa.gov.uk

Financial Ombudsman Service

The FOS helps settle individual disputes between businesses providing financial services and their customers. It was set up by parliament to do this – as independent experts – and its service is free to consumers. The FOS can consider complaints about a wide range of financial matters – from insurance and mortgages to investments and credit.

0845 080 1800/www.fos.org.uk

Association of British Insurers

The ABI is the trade association representing the UK's insurance industry. It provides information to consumers on a wide range of insurance issues.

020 7600 3333/www.abi.org.uk

Pensions
Pension Protection Fund

The Pension Protection Fund (PPF) was set up in April 2005 to protect you if your employer goes bust and its pension scheme can no longer afford to pay you your promised pension. It can provide details of the compensation scheme and protection in place for final-salary scheme members.

0845 600 2541/www.pensionprotectionfund.org.uk

Pensions Ombudsman

The Pensions Ombudsman investigates and decides complaints and disputes about the way that pension schemes are run.

020 7634 9144/www.pensions-ombudsman.org.uk

The Pensions Regulator

Regulator of work-based pensions with powers to investigate schemes.

0870 606 3636/www.thepensionsregulator.gov.uk

The Pension Service

Part of the Department for Work and Pensions, this is a government service with information about pensions and benefits for retired people and those planning their retirement.

0845 6060 265/www.thepensionservice.gov.uk

Pensions Tracing Service

Free service to trace old pension schemes. Available through The Pension Service website: www.thepensionservice.gov.uk
0845 6002 537

HM Revenue & Customs

Contact HMRC for information about the tax treatment of pensions as well as details of the self-assessment process for claiming higher-rate tax relief.

0115 974 1600/www.hmrc.gov.uk/pensionschemes

Advice

IFA Promotion

Provides personal finance information as well as a service to find an independent financial adviser in your local area.

0800 085 3250/www.unbiased.co.uk

Association of Private Client Investment Managers and Stockbrokers

Provides general information on share dealing. Its directory of members can help you find an investment manager or stockbroker who will meet your needs.

020 7247 7080/www.apcims.co.uk

The Pensions Advisory Service

The Pensions Advisory Service is an independent non-profit organisation that provides free information, advice and guidance on the whole spectrum of pensions, covering state, company, personal and stakeholder schemes.

Helpline: 0845 601 2923 (calls are charged at local rates)

www.pensionsadvisoryservice.org.uk

Charities

Age Concern

Information and advice on issues affecting people in their 50s and beyond, including taking retirement income and financial help in retirement.

0800 009966/www.ageconcern.org.uk

Help the Aged

Advice and support for people in and approaching retirement.

020 7278 1114/www.helptheaged.org.uk

Citizens Advice

A registered charity providing free, independent and confidential advice to help people resolve their legal and money problems, including debt problems. Visit www.citizensadvice.org.uk. The charity also provides practical, up-to-date information on a wide range of topics, including benefits and housing, debt and tax issues through its other website www. adviceguide.org.uk.

Investment

Investment Management Association

This UK trade body has a range of guides and fact sheets for investors. Its website also has tools to help you 'find a fund manager' and 'find a fund' to suit you.

020 7831 0895/www.investmentuk.org

Association of Investment Companies

The AIC is the trade organisation for the closed-ended investment company industry. It represents a broad range of closed-ended investment companies, incorporating investment trusts, offshore closed-ended investment companies, venture capital trusts (VCTs), AIM traded investment companies and a Euronext company. Its website provides a comprehensive guide to investment companies and a useful search.

020 7282 5555/www.theaic.co.uk

Association of Friendly Societies

The AFS represents the friendly society movement, and has over 50 members. Between them, these organisations manage the savings and investments of over 4.5 million people, and have total funds under management of around £15 billion. Friendly societies were established to encourage self-help and personal responsibility and to enable people with limited financial resources to improve their economic status. They don't have shareholders, which means the full benefits of the products are passed on to their customers.

0161 952 5051/www.afs.org.uk

Useful personal finance websites

www.moneyfacts.co.uk

An independent and unbiased website that will help you to make informed decisions on your personal finances. It's free Best Buy charts give a unique snapshot of the best products available in the market.

www.trustnet.com

Trustnet is a free website devoted exclusively to research into investment funds and investment trusts. It has a range of educational material, plus detailed information on collective investment vehicles.

Index